Luminescent
BANNER DESIGNS

Marie E. Pierce-Ruhland Koehlinger

SAINT LOUIS

Copyright © 1998 Concordia Publishing House
3558 S. Jefferson Avenue, St. Louis, MO 63118-3968
Manufactured in the United States of America

Purchasers of this product may reproduce designs for the completion of projects.

1 2 3 4 5 6 7 8 9 10   07 06 05 04 03 02 01 00 99 98

CONTENTS

ACKNOWLEDGMENTS

I have many people to thank for helping me develop this book. Rev. Craig Otto, a pastor and an ecclesiastical artist, allowed me to include two of his designs. They appear on pages 38 and 40. It was an honor to work with such a fine artist, even if it was for only a brief time.

Since I am not a typist, several people gave up their time—and their sleep—to make the manuscript presentable. My mother, Harriet Pierce-Ruhland, was my first typist and editor. She offered valuable insights from a layperson's perspective to help me communicate more effectively with someone unfamiliar with this banner-making technique. For that, I am grateful. Both she and my dad, Richard, have been a source of inspiration and encouragement for my artwork.

Barbara and David Flushing and Iris Rahubka helped me develop fonts for the banners. These friends spent numerous hours bringing the message of each banner to life. Without their efforts, the banners would lie quietly on the page. Barbara and David are among the most creative people I know, and they offered wonderful ideas to enhance the messages of the banners. They also provided encouragement for my work.

Lynne Strian, another source of encouragement, survived hours at the computer, entering countless revisions. An idea factory with fantastic organizational skills, she kept me motivated when I had reached the end of my rope. Without her, this book wouldn't exist.

I would be remiss not to mention my husband, Vern, and our three sons—Benjamin, Peter, and Zachary—who endured my extended use of the dining room table as well as less of my time. Vern gave me frank opinions on my designs and often inspired better banners. He also edited the manuscript. A big thank you to him!

But the inspiration behind this book is the Lord, who has blessed me beyond words. His Word is alive and active, and it brought images to my mind to illustrate His message on the banners. These banner designs are my witness to you, dear reader, of an awesome and loving God. He desires that each of us will grow in our relationship with Him so we may know the outpouring of His love and blessings. He loves us so much that He sent His Son, Jesus, to stretch out His arms and die to take away our sins. Without this great act of love on God's part, our sins would eternally separate us from Him.

I pray that these banner designs will bring out these messages both to you and to those for whom you make them.

INTRODUCTION

Fabrics are glorious! This book will open the door to the wide variety of beautiful fibers, colors, and textures that can enhance the beauty of your church banners, paraments, and clerical furnishings and provide them with a new dimension. This book also will introduce you to a new technique for making banners. A few sample designs will introduce you to the technique before you attempt the full-size banners. The designs in this book introduce a new art form called *luminescent* banners.

WHAT ARE *Luminescent* Banners?

Luminescent banners differ from other banners in regard to the fabrics used (not the traditional felt) and the adherent (not glue). The concept of luminescent banners developed because glue proved to be an inadequate adherent for a detailed design. In this art form, the adherent does not interfere with the finished product by puckering, discoloring, or spotting the fabric.

The technique used in luminescent banners accommodates designs with pieces small enough to fit under a fingernail. These pieces actually could be considered elements of a fabric mosaic. Because of the adherent and the technique, the fabric is extremely stable at any size and does not fray at the edges. The beauty of this technique is the maintenance of the integrity of each fabric when applied to the surface of the banner.

WHY ARE THESE BANNERS CALLED *Luminescent*?

Because this technique allows the designer to use nearly every type of fabric, it opens up banner design to those fabrics filled with light-reflective qualities. These include metallics, silks, silkies, satins, suedes, and so on. Each fabric has its own distinct "personality." It is exciting to become acquainted with each fabric's potential and apply it to its fullest on the finished banner. Even though the fabrics are applied flat, at times they give the illusion of being three-dimensional. Luminescent banners constantly catch light from different sources and appear to be "alive."

The techniques developed in this art form lend themselves to the construction of banners and paraments. With this technique, paraments take on a new role in the worship setting. The parament no longer has to be limited to a spot of color on the altar, pulpit, or lectern. The paraments can display seasonal symbolism on prominent wall space, such as on either side of the altar, where banners might look out of place.

Imagine during Lent looking into the face of Christ as He anticipates His sacrifice. His face, full of love, reveals His willingness to give up His life to win our salvation. This cannot be achieved in a small bookmark on the lectern or pulpit. Realism in church banners can be achieved as never before with this art form. And the realism can be intense because it is done on a large scale.

What Skills Are Required?

The skills necessary to make luminescent banners are patience, a steady hand for tracing and cutting, and careful attention to directions. The time it takes to make a banner lessens with experience. The baptismal banner on page 88 used to take four hours to construct. Each banner now takes two or three hours of labor to complete. (These banners cost about $3.00 each to make.)

Supplies

The following items are suggested to help you construct luminescent banners.

- A Pilot Precise Rolling Ball Pen—Extra Fine or a similar writing tool.

- Therm O Web HeatnBond lightweight and heavyweight paper (found in fabric stores).

- A light source behind a translucent flat surface. This will be used to trace pattern pieces onto the HeatnBond paper. This light source can be natural (daylight behind a windowpane) or electrical (fluorescent tubes arranged behind a glass surface). The size of the surface is determined by the size of the banner. The larger the lighted surface, the easier it is to manage large pattern pieces.

- Sharp, pointed 6″ scissors. Fiskars or Ginghers are recommended.

- A clean iron with multiple settings. *No steam will be used.*

- A hard, *flat* surface without texture or seams that can withstand the heat of an iron. (An ironing board has too much padding to bond fabrics thoroughly.) A countertop is fine for small banners. You can use your dining room table for large banners. To protect your table, purchase a 4′ × 8′ sheet of plywood (for stability) and a sheet of bathroom Masonite wall- board with a *smooth* white coating (often used in shower stalls). The Masonite will protect the fabric from snags.

- Masonite wallboard also can be cut into 12″ widths. These are effective tools when working on a flat surface with seams (i.e., a kitchen countertop with a seam or a Ping-Pong table with a center seam). Just slide the board over the seam between the banner and the flat surface. Thus ironing on the banner will not be marred by the unevenness of the seam.

- Other tools (all are useful but not necessary to complete the banners): right angle/rule, cellophane tape, T-shaped pins (to maneuver fabric pieces into place), X-Acto knife, finger trolley (Pix brand), drafting triangles, art white erasers, and rolls of white paper (to make the pattern). Tablecloth paper on a roll works well to make the pattern. Select the width of the roll based on the size of the banner. For example, if you are making a large banner for the front of your church, you probably will want to use 48″ wide paper. Paper also can be taped together to make a wider pattern.

- And finally, fabric! Shop to your heart's content. Once I arrived at the fabric store counter with a brilliant green silk, a hot pink satin, a purple metallic, a deep gold satin, and an odd array of brightly colored to dull fabrics. A woman who stood nearby with her smartly coordinated fabric selection was trying hard not to show her concern for my taste. I broke the silence by assuring her that my selections were not for wearing. She smiled in relief!

After you begin making luminescent banners, you will begin to see what you thought to be quite ordinary things in new ways. You will view your favorite fabric store as a giant paint pallet from which you can build banners that glisten with exclamation or softly express the messages you arrange on them. People probably will not look at you in the same way either.

Constructing Luminescent Banners

Begin with the Sampler Designs

Before you tackle one of the full-size banner designs, practice on one of the smaller sampler designs. Select from the designs on pages 13, 16, 19, and 22. These first designs include specific directions regarding color and layering to help you interpret the pattern. The full-size banner designs will not include all these details. It might prove helpful to photocopy the design from this book and pencil notes on the pattern to help you prepare and assemble the separate design elements. The sampler design on page 22 introduces a lacing technique that is used on several of the full-size banners.

As you "read" the designs, remember that the elements are layered on the background fabric. In some instances, you may not even see the background fabric because it's covered by large blocks of decorative fabric. Throughout the book, design elements that have a narrow double-line outline are elements adhered to black or other dark fabric. This dark outline allows the luminescent qualities of the decorative fabrics on top to receive the focus. In general this dark fabric outline is one large piece of fabric. The colored fabrics on top may have shapes cut out to allow the dark fabric beneath to outline still other areas of the design.

Enlarging the Design

To enlarge a banner design, use a photocopier for small incremental increases in size. Most full-service copy centers have photocopy machines that reproduce blueprints. This offers many possibilities for the banner maker. If you want to enlarge the design beyond a photocopier's capacity, photocopy the design onto a transparency and project the image onto a wall. Adjust the image size to the dimensions of the finished banner by moving the projector forward or backward. Then trace the projected image onto tablecloth paper to make the pattern. Use this pattern to trace the individual design elements onto HeatnBond paper. *Note:* Project the reverse of the design or you will need to reverse the pattern on the light source surface when you trace the individual pattern pieces.

The designs in this book can be enlarged to any size you feel comfortable working with, but keep in mind that the dark outline fabric should not extend more than ¼" beyond the colorful fabrics on top. An outline of ⅛" is best.

Preparing the Pattern

After you have photocopied the design (or enlarged it), follow these basic directions to complete the pattern for the sampler banners or for the full-size banners. Each banner design also will include special directions regarding unique features or construction techniques.

To prepare the pattern

1. *Reverse* the photocopied design on the light source surface. If you do not, you will have a mirror image when you complete the banner. With the sampler designs, it will not make a difference; however, for the full-size banners, it is essential to reverse the design before tracing.

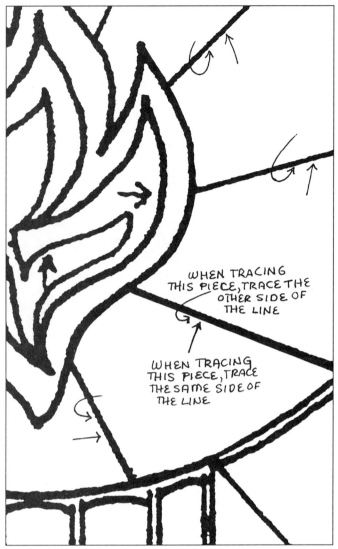

WHEN TRACING
THIS PIECE, TRACE THE
OTHER SIDE OF
THE LINE

WHEN TRACING
THIS PIECE, TRACE
THE SAME SIDE OF
THE LINE

1 *When tracing the pattern, trace the same "side" of the line to ensure that the pieces fit.*

2. *Tape* the design in place on the light source surface.

3. *Trace* the design onto white paper or, for larger projects, onto tablecloth paper. *Never trace the design directly onto the HeatnBond paper.* When you enlarge the patterns from this book, the line will become thicker. Trace the side of the line that will *increase* the size of the colored area and *decrease* the black line outlining that color. Generally, this would be the outside "edge" of the line. Make sure that you always trace the same edge, though, so individual design elements fit together (see diagram 1).

Constructing the Banner Background

To construct the background fabric (the single fabric on which all the separate design elements will be layered), first determine the finished width of the banner. Then add 2″ to each side. Place the fabric wrong side down, fold the edges in toward the middle 2″, and iron flat to make a crease.

Now measure the distance between the two sides and add ½″. Measure the distance from the top to the bottom and add ½″. Cut lining fabric to these dimensions. Sew the right side of the lining to the right side of the background fabric with ¼″ seams. Leave a section open at the bottom. Iron the seam open.

Turn the banner background fabric right side out. Baste the opening close. Iron flat to prepare it for the application of the design elements.

Preparing the Design Elements

Determine which fabrics you will use for each element of the design. Note the colors and highlight directions on a photocopy of the design. Once you have decided on fabrics, follow the directions on the HeatnBond paper to match the correct weight of paper to the fabrics you have chosen.

Tape the traced design to the light source surface. Secure the appropriate weight of HeatnBond paper smooth side up (pebbly side down) over the individual design element to be traced. Use an extra-fine point pen to trace precisely over every line or curve. (For long lines, use a small, maneuverable ruler or a drafting triangle. For curves, use a steady hand.) If you find you have strayed, make "railroad tracks" where you do not want to cut and redraw the line from where you began to stray. Don't start over. Where

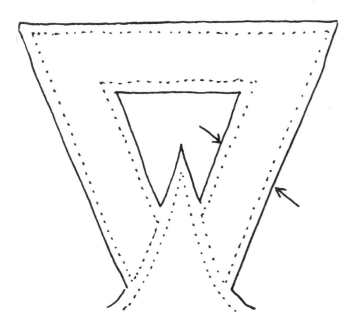

2 *Trace the outermost line for cutout sections.*

most often with the weft of the fabric from selvage to selvage). Set your iron on the lower end of "steam," but *do not* use steam. Bond the pattern piece to the fabric by applying the iron flat against the paper for two to three seconds. This will bond the fabric and the HeatnBond paper together. Lift the iron to check that there are no wrinkles or creases, then lightly reapply the iron to the surface in a circular motion. Progress to a firm pressure with the iron to ensure all the adherent is melted and secured to the fabric. If the paper does not adhere evenly, the cut edges of the fabric will fray. You can tell if the fabric and the paper are adhered tightly with these tests:

- Are there areas of light and dark? If so, the lighter areas are not ironed completely.
- Can you run a fingernail or a finger trolley around the pattern piece and bring the HeatnBond paper up easily? If so, iron the edges again.

Cut the individual design elements from the fabric, leaving a ⅛″ to ¼″ margin around the HeatnBond paper. (The extra fabric ensures that no adherent will gum up your iron if you use the remaining "scrap" fabric on another project.)

cutouts occur, trace only the outermost line (see diagram 2).

After you have traced all the separate elements onto HeatnBond paper, cut out the elements, leaving a ⅛″ to ¼″ margin around the traced lines. *Do not cut on the line at this point! Do not cut closer to the line than ⅛″.*

Mark all the pattern pieces with a number, the appropriate fabric and/or color, and the highlight direction. Number the corresponding section on an intact photocopy of the design so you can assemble the pieces correctly.

To adhere the pattern pieces to the fabric, first place the fabric right side down (wrong side up). Lay the Heatn-Bond pattern piece smooth side up on top of the fabric. Align the directional arrow with the highlight of the fabric (which is

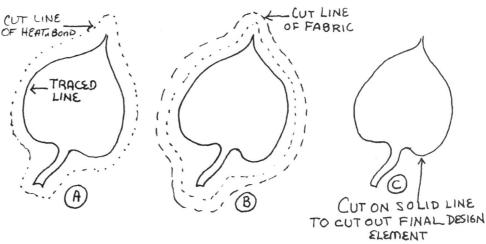

3 *These are the stages of cutting the individual design elements. The solid line represents the actual traced pattern. Step A represents the element after the piece is traced onto HeatnBond paper and cut out. Step B represents the element after the HeatnBond pattern piece has been bonded to fabric and cut out. Step C represents the final design element, cut from the fabric along the solid line and ready to be bonded to the banner background.*

9

Finally, after all the pattern pieces have been adhered to fabric, cut out the design elements. Because cutting is so important to the beauty of the luminescent banner, don't assume that this is a simple task. The line you cut is the line you will see on the finished product. The dark outline fabric will accentuate this perfect or imperfect line. Cutting requires patience and precision, so take your pointed, sharp-edged scissors and get comfortable. Work under a good light source. Cut out each piece slowly and carefully. *Stay on the traced line!*

When cutting, keep the blades of the scissors in contact with the fabric as you open the scissors to cut. To remove the blade from the surface or to carelessly replace the blade on the line causes a "shark-tooth" effect.

Do not shortchange corners. Instead, overcut the corners (see diagram 4). This ensures a clean appearance for your finished banner.

When cutting a curve, be careful to cut in a curved line, not a series of small straight cuts. A curved line takes coordination. If you are left-handed, cut a curve clockwise; if you are

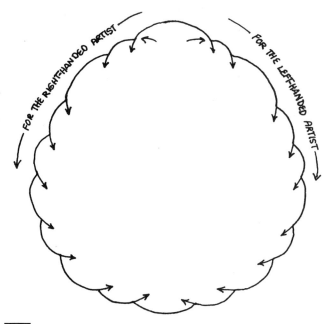

5 *Cutting a curve.*

right-handed, cut a curve counterclockwise (see diagram 5). Whichever is your preferred hand, hold the pattern piece in the opposite hand and move it toward your preferred hand, which is cutting at a smooth, consistent speed.

When cutting out the inside of a letter or of a design element, cut in the center of the piece if the hole is large enough, then cut toward a corner. Overcut into the corner so changing direction is clean and not shark-toothed. If the letter or design element is too small to pierce the center cleanly with a scissors, use either an X-Acto knife and a cutting board or cut through the side to the center of the element. When the piece is ironed down, it will "heal." Try to cut with the grain of the fabric or with the highlight direction (parallel to the arrow). When ironing the side that has been cut, or when ironing a corner that has been overcut, be careful not to overlap the two edges. Instead, the edges should butt up against each other.

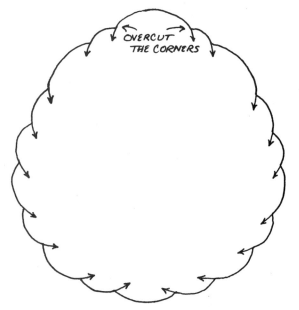

4 *When cutting corners or curves, cut past the change of direction, then pick up the line again. When the piece is adhered to the background or outline fabric, the "extra" cut will be masked.*

ASSEMBLING THE DESIGN

Now that all the individual design elements have been traced, bonded, and cut out from the fabric, it's time to assemble the banner.

Make sure the background fabric is ironed flat. Double-check the design in the book to verify the order in which the separate elements need to be adhered. Practice positioning the elements first to ensure that the pieces fit together to make the finished banner. If necessary, trim pieces to correct any imperfections and to ensure a tight fit. Retrace and cut out any piece that does not fit properly.

Once you are satisfied with the overall look, carefully remove the top layers. Remove the HeatnBond paper from the bottom "layer" of the design. Position this design element on the background fabric. Set the iron between 5 and 6 and carefully iron this layer in place. Be certain that all the edges are secure. It is difficult to re-iron the bottom layer once the other layers of fabric have been added.

Now that the bottom layer has been adhered to the background fabric, add the next layer of design elements. Tack the individual pieces in place by gently applying heat to a part of each element. Be careful because too much pressure on some fabrics will dimple the cloth. After each piece is secured, re-check position. If any piece isn't positioned correctly, carefully reposition the piece. (See page 12 for directions to reposition design elements.)

After you have tacked all the design elements in place, select a *used* sheet of HeatnBond paper, one that has *no adhesive*. (You can rub off any cooled adherent. If you do not remove all the adherent and you are working with permeable fabrics, you might apply adherent to the fabrics and soil them.) Place the used HeatnBond paper *shiny side down* on the assembled banner pieces. Iron in a slow circular motion, applying an even amount of pressure. Occasionally lift the paper (after allowing it to cool) to run a fingernail or finger trolley around the edges of the design element to check for adherence. Carefully go over the entire surface of the banner to make sure all design elements are adhered.

SPECIAL NOTES

The following are some useful tips to keep in mind when constructing luminescent banners.

- Tracing an incorrect line happens, especially when dealing with small pieces. Don't try to start over; instead, put "railroad tracks" over the incorrect line and draw the correct one.

- The arrows in the designs represent one option for how the highlight in the fabric might be positioned in the final design. Feel free to develop your own highlight scheme.

- The moiré stripe usually travels the length of the fabric, not from selvage to selvage. When using moiré, the arrow on the design parallels the moiré stripe.

- It's best to iron on a flat, seamless surface. If you do not have access to such a surface, cut a length of Masonite (not less than 12″ long) to place under the banner. When you iron your design elements to the background fabric, place the board under the fabric to make a hard, flat surface that will protect the fabrics.

- If the HeatnBond paper doesn't appear to be sticking well, turn up the iron setting in small increments until the adhesive works properly.

- If the fabric is curling or shrinking under your iron, turn down the iron setting in small increments. Settings listed in this book are conservative; more than likely, you will need more heat rather than less.

- If the HeatnBond paper comes loose from the fabric before you finish cutting the shape, carefully realign it and re-iron it.

- Always allow the HeatnBond paper to cool before removing it from the fabric, especially when using the used HeatnBond paper to adhere the design elements in their final positions. If you don't and adherent has seeped through the fabric to the paper, you may pull up parts of the design and/or permanently warp fabrics such as silks or silkies.

- If you need to remove an incorrectly positioned design element, apply heat to the piece to soften the adherent, then peel it off. You may need to retrace the piece and cut it out. Silk especially warps when even a small corner is lifted while it is still warm. It cannot be reshaped and must be replaced.

- When working with silk, it is best not to tack the design elements. It usually will result in dimpled fabric that needs to be removed and replaced. Instead, position the design elements and lay a used sheet of HeatnBond paper over the pieces. Hold the paper over those elements that are correctly positioned and reach underneath the paper with a finger trolley or X-Acto knife to maneuver other pieces into position. Then iron the pieces in place.

- If you remove a design element and discover it has stained the banner, carefully use a single-edged razor to "shave" the soiled fibers from the surface. This can be done even on white fabric.

- If the edges of the fabric ruffle while ironing a design element onto the background fabric, don't panic. Carefully remove the design element. Cut a piece of HeatnBond paper, place it under the ruffled edge, and adhere it. Now remove the HeatnBond paper, arrange the design element on the background fabric, and carefully re-adhere, paying special attention to the ruffled edge.

- If you ruffle the edge of silk or lamé fabric, you must remove the design element and remake that particular piece.

- If a decorative fabric you have chosen for a design element is too thin and the dark outline fabric shows through, line the design element with white cotton. To do this, trace the design element on heavy HeatnBond paper and iron it to the cotton lining fabric. Now adhere the decorative fabric piece to the cotton lining. Cut out the final design piece. You will adhere the cotton lining to the dark outline fabric.

- If you cannot find the right color for a design element, dye your own fabrics with Rit fabric dye. Even synthetics will dye to some degree. You can mix colors, if necessary, to make the desired hue. Use white fabrics or, for deeper values, use a fabric that comes close to the finished color. You can use dark brown Rit fabric dye on the fabric for the eagle on the wedding banner (page 79). When using the dye on synthetic fabrics, do not rinse the fabric. This reduces the intensity of the color. It's best to dry the fabric outside, unless you have a place where you won't damage floors or carpets as the stain drips.

- To clean a dirty iron, put dry baking soda on an old cotton towel. Set the iron on its hottest setting (linen), then rub and twist the iron on the towel until it is clean.

You are now ready to construct and design banners that will enhance worship services for years to come. When your efforts are to God's glory, you and your endeavors will be blessed. May He accentuate your gifts as you give back to Him what He first gave you to the glory of His holy name!

SAMPLER DESIGN A • CROWN AND CROSS

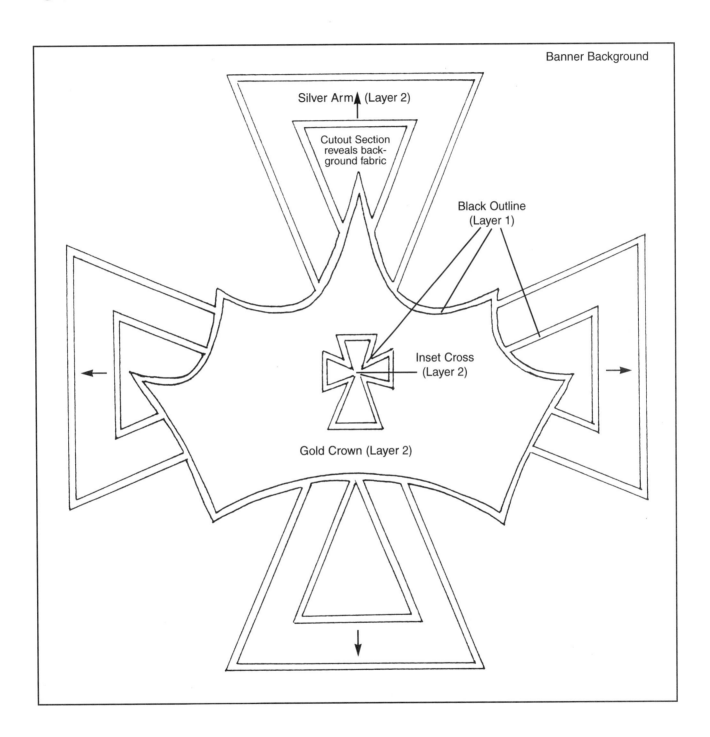

Banner Background

Silver Arm (Layer 2)

Cutout Section reveals background fabric

Black Outline (Layer 1)

Inset Cross (Layer 2)

Gold Crown (Layer 2)

SUGGESTED FABRIC AND COLORS

For all the banners in this book, use a cotton or a cotton blend for the background fabric. The fabric you choose should be heavy enough to support the decorative fabrics applied to it. A cotton blend will resist wrinkling. Pure linens hold wrinkles that can mar the finished banner. Do not use knits or polyesters because they will sag and droop.

- For the background fabric for this sampler, use green, red, or blue cotton or a cotton blend.
- For the dark outline of the crown and cross, use black cotton-poly broadcloth.
- For the arms of the cross, use silver lamé.
- For the crown, use any metallic gold fabric.
- For the inset cross, use the same fabric as the background fabric.

MAKING THE DESIGN ELEMENTS

TRACING

Trace the outline of the crown and cross onto heavyweight HeatnBond paper. This will be layer 1 of the banner design. This is actually one piece with the centers of the arms of the cross cut out. The shape will look like diagram 1. Remember to trace the outermost line of the cutout sections. The inner line actually identifies the shape of the design element that will be layered on top of the dark outline fabric (see diagram 2).

Next, trace each arm of the cross. Use lightweight HeatnBond paper for lamés or heavyweight HeatnBond paper for metallic fabrics. The arm pieces, along with the crown and inset cross, will be layer 2 of the finished banner (see diagram 3). In the middle of each arm, write the color of the fabric and the arm

1 *The "shape" of the black outline fabric.*

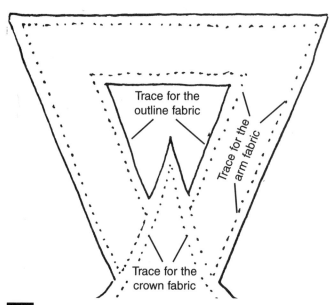

2 *Trace the outermost line in cutout sections.*

position, then draw an arrow to indicate the direction of the highlight. To conserve HeatnBond paper as well as fabric, line up the highlight arrows of pieces going on the same fabric and trace them as closely together as possible (see diagram 4).

Trace the crown. If you use lamé for the crown, use lightweight HeatnBond paper. Again, trace the outermost line of the cutout for the inset cross. Remember to mark the

14

3 *The "shape" of the arm, crown, and inset cross design elements.*

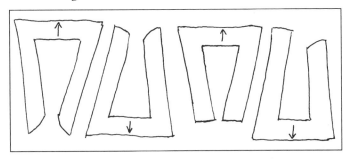

4 *Position pieces to conserve HeatnBond paper and fabric.*

color and highlight direction.

Finally, trace the inset cross onto another piece of heavyweight HeatnBond paper.

CUTTING OUT THE DESIGN ELEMENT PATTERNS

Cut out the patterns leaving a ⅛″ to ¼″ margin around the lines. *Do not cut on the line at this point!*

BONDING THE DESIGN ELEMENTS

Find the smallest piece of fabric that is big enough for each design element. Place it face down or wrong side up on your work surface. Place the HeatnBond paper pattern smooth side up on top of the fabric. Line up the arrow with the highlight of the fabric. Bond the pattern to the fabric. Check the edges for adherence.

CUTTING OUT THE FINAL DESIGN ELEMENTS

Cut out the individual design elements from the fabric, leaving a ⅛″ to ¼″ margin around the HeatnBond paper. Then get comfortable and cut out each element along the actual line of the pattern.

ASSEMBLING THE BANNER

Construct the banner background fabric and iron it. Remove the HeatnBond paper from the black outline of the crown and cross. Position it on the background fabric. Set your iron between 5 and 6 and carefully iron the outline in place. Be certain that all the edges are secure. It is difficult to re-iron this bottom layer after the decorative fabrics have been adhered on top. You run the risk of ruining these finer fabrics.

Remove the HeatnBond paper from the remaining design elements. Place each piece on top of the black outline in its proper position. Make sure the design elements have been cut correctly and fit together well. If necessary, trim to correct any imperfections. Retrace and cut out any piece that does not fit properly.

Tack the individual design elements in place. After each piece is secured, re-check positioning. If any piece is not placed correctly, carefully remove the element and reposition it.

Once all the design elements are in position, place a sheet of *used* HeatnBond paper (one that has no adhesive) *shiny side down* on the assembled banner. Press evenly in a slow circular motion with the iron. Occasionally lift the paper (after allowing it to cool) to check the fabric for secure edges.

SAMPLER DESIGN B • BAPTISMAL SHELL

Banner Background

Black Outline
(Layer 1)

Silver Fabric
(Layer 2)

Omit on shells
5" or smaller

SUGGESTED FABRIC AND COLORS

- For the background fabric, use a cotton or a cotton blend in any color.
- For the dark outline of the shell, use a black or navy cotton-poly blend.
- For the outer edge of the shell, use silver fabric with directional highlights.
- For the separate pieces of the inner shell, use nondirectional silver fabric.

MAKING THE DESIGN ELEMENTS

Trace the outline of the shell onto HeatnBond paper (see diagram 1).

Next, trace the "ring" that outlines the smaller, separate shell pieces (see diagram 2). Do not cut out the center portion of the ring until after it is bonded to the fabric. The extra paper will help to stabilize this design element as it is bonded to the fabric.

Finally, trace the separate shell sections. Number each section and add arrows to indicate highlight direction (see diagram 3).

Once all the elements have been traced onto HeatnBond paper and cut out (remember the extra margin around the actual pattern line), bond the pieces to the appropriate fabric. Make sure the arrows line up with the highlight of the fabric.

Cut out the elements from the fabric, again leaving the extra margin around the HeatnBond paper. Now cut out the final design elements. Make sure to overcut each curve on the outline fabric and the outer ring of the shell to ensure clean edges on the finished banner.

1 *The "shape" of the outline fabric.*

2 *The "shape" of the outer ring.*

3 *The "shape" of the inner shell pieces.*

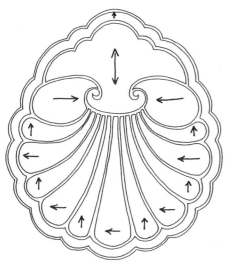

4 *The numbers indicate the order of placement and the dots indicate the best place to tack each piece.*

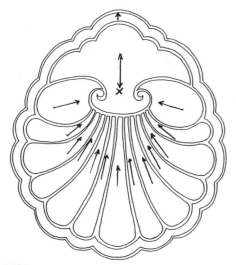

5 *A vertical/horizontal highlight scheme.*

6 *A radiating highlight scheme.*

ASSEMBLING THE BANNER

Construct the background fabric and iron it. Remove the HeatnBond paper from the outline fabric. Place the outline fabric on the background and iron it securely. Check the edges for adherence.

Next, place the outer ring of the shell and the individual sections of the inner shell in position. Check for fit. Tack the outer ring and the large top section of the inner shell in place. Arrange the smaller shell sections below the top section, starting from the center and going out in both directions as indicated by the numbers in diagram 4. Allow a narrow black outline to show between each section. Use a finger trolley or X-Acto knife to move the sections into position. Tack each section in place. The dots in diagram 4 show suggested places to tack each section. (If the fabric is curling, position the narrow ends of each piece evenly around the base of the top section and tack lightly. Then uncurl each piece and tack the outer edge.)

When every piece has been tacked in position, lay a used sheet of HeatnBond paper over all the design elements. (Remember to check for adherent left on the paper and rub it off.) Iron firmly in a circular motion to adhere all the elements. Check the edges for adherence and re-iron any loose areas.

SPECIAL NOTES

This design can be reduced to 3½″ or magnified to 12″ or larger. If you wish to make it the size shown in the pattern or smaller, iron the HeatnBond pattern on the silver fabric without regard to highlight direction. For a small 4″ or 5″ shell, trace and cut the entire shell on nondirectional silver fabric. Omit the outer ring of the shell on smaller banners.

You can choose from three highlight schemes when constructing this banner design. First, you can trace the element as a single piece and the direction is fixed by the fabric. Second, you can alternate the direction of the highlights between vertical and horizontal (see diagram 5). Third, the highlight of each section of the shell can radiate from a single fixed point (see diagram 6). This final option works best in a large format.

SAMPLER DESIGN C • CROSS

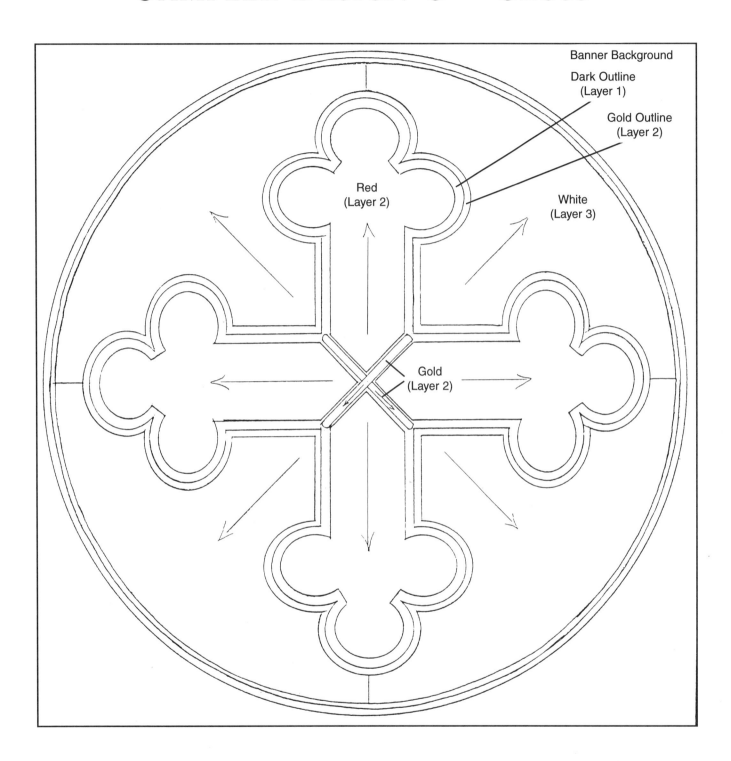

Banner Background

Dark Outline
(Layer 1)

Gold Outline
(Layer 2)

Red
(Layer 2)

White
(Layer 3)

Gold
(Layer 2)

Suggested Fabric and Colors

- The background fabric for this sampler should be red cotton.
- The first layer of the cross outline should be a black cotton-poly blend.
- Use gold lamé for the second layer of the cross outline (just inside the black outline).
- Use white satin for the four sections surrounding the cross (just inside the double outline).
- For the arms of the cross, use red silk or moiré.
- For the center crosspiece, use the same gold lamé as the second outline.

1 The "shape" of the black outline fabric.

Making the Design Elements

This is a more complicated layering system. Pay careful attention to the way the elements fit together, especially the cutout section of the gold lamé outline piece.

First, trace the two layers of the outline. Diagram 1 represents the shape of the outline to be bonded to the black fabric. Diagram 2 represents the shape of the outline to be bonded to the gold fabric.

Second, trace the four sections of the circle. If you trace the separate sections as shown in diagram 3, you will conserve HeatnBond paper and fabric.

Third, trace the arms of the cross. Again, trace the sections as shown in diagram 4 to use paper and fabric efficiently. Finally, trace the center crosspieces.

Number each section and add arrows to indicate highlight direction. The numbering system in the diagrams is only one way to do this (all the number 1s fit together, all the number 2s, etc.).

Cut out the pattern pieces from the HeatnBond paper. Adhere the patterns to the proper fabrics, aligning the arrows with the highlight. Cut out the final design elements. It's important to be precise as you cut out these pieces because of the more complicated layering and the adjoining edges of the white sections of the circle.

2 The "shape" of the gold outline fabric.

3 Position the circle sections to conserve HeatnBond paper and fabric.

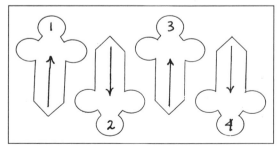

4 Position the arms to conserve HeatnBond paper and fabric.

20

ASSEMBLING THE BANNER

Construct the background fabric. Adhere the black outline (layer 1) to the background fabric. Tack the gold outline (layer 2) on the black outline. Make sure there is a uniform black outline around the perimeter. Place a sheet of used HeatnBond paper on top of these layers and iron flat. Make sure the gold fabric is ironed securely.

Next, place the four white sections just inside the gold circle. The gold outline should be the same width as the black outline. The white sections also will emphasize the double outline of the cross arms. Make sure there is no gap nor overlap of the white sections where they butt up to each other over the ends of the cross (indicated by the arrows in diagram 5). Place a sheet of used HeatnBond paper over the design elements and bond them in place.

Now lay the red cross arms on the black fabric inside the cutout section of the gold fabric. The points of each arm will leave a gap at the center of the cross (see diagram 6). Place a sheet of used HeatnBond paper over the top of the arm pieces and bond them in place.

Finally, position the two small strips of gold fabric in the gap between the four cross arms. Overlap the pieces in the center as shown. Iron in place. Check all edges and re-iron as necessary.

5   *Make sure the edges of the white sections do not overlap.*

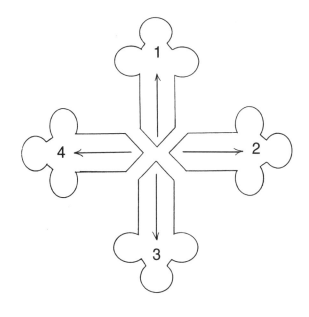

6   *Leave a uniform gap in the center of the cross arms.*

21

SAMPLER DESIGN D • BUTTERFLY

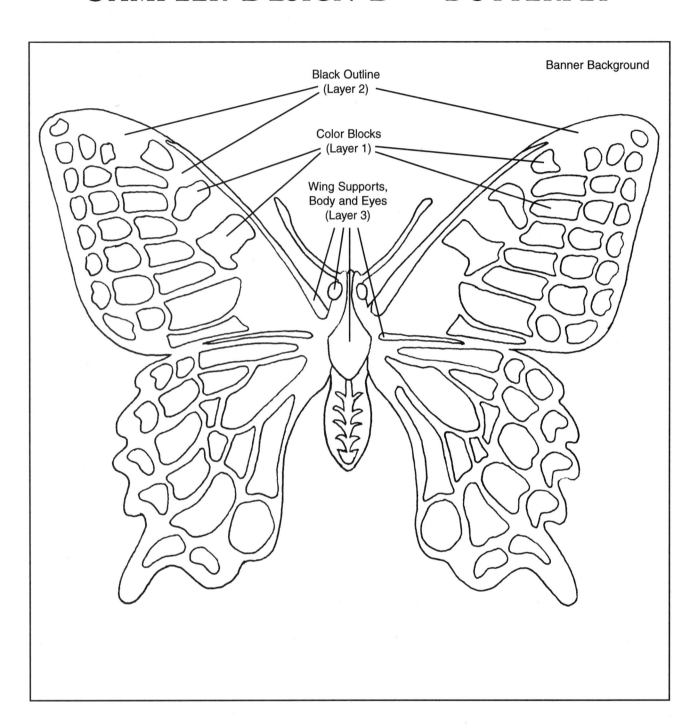

Banner Background

Black Outline
(Layer 2)

Color Blocks
(Layer 1)

Wing Supports,
Body and Eyes
(Layer 3)

ONE LAST TECHNIQUE

The previous three designs employ nearly every technique necessary to complete luminescent banners. But one technique is different from the rest. The results are worth the time and practice needed to learn it. This "lacing technique" is especially useful for this butterfly design or when constructing a bunch of grapes. You will use the technique to construct the banners on pages 34, 44, and 82. This technique ensures the charm and integrity of color in the design. It is an option any time a light color is placed over the black or dark outline fabric. (A second option is to line the decorative fabric with white cotton.)

1 *The "shape" of the black outline fabric.*

SUGGESTED FABRIC AND COLORS

- The background fabric for this sampler should be any complimentary color in a cotton or cotton blend.

- For the wing outline, which includes the antennae, use black cotton-poly broadcloth.

- Choose bright colors for the wing sections. Possibilities include a bright yellow silkie with a tone-on-tone print, a bright blue metallic, or a bright red silkie.

- For the body, use dark brown lightweight cotton.

- The wing supports can be medium gray cotton.

- Use nondirectional metallic green for the eyes.

MAKING THE DESIGN ELEMENTS

If necessary, enlarge the design so it is comfortable to work with. Trace the entire butterfly—around the body, antennae, and wings. Also trace all the cutout sections of the wings (see diagram 1). Adhere the HeatnBond pattern to the black broadcloth.

Now cut out the butterfly shape, including all the wing cutouts. You may want to use an X-Acto knife for the smaller cutouts. Make sure to use a flat, firm surface when using an X-Acto knife so the fabric is cut smoothly. When you finish cutting out the butterfly, the result will be a black butterfly with holes where the wing colors will be placed.

Each section of wing cutouts will be a different color and highlight direction (see diagram 2). Consult books about butterflies for other color combinations. First, plot where the colors you have chosen will appear. Then make HeatnBond paper patterns that will cover those sections on both wings. Bond it to the appropriate fabric, paying careful attention to the highlight direction. Cut out the

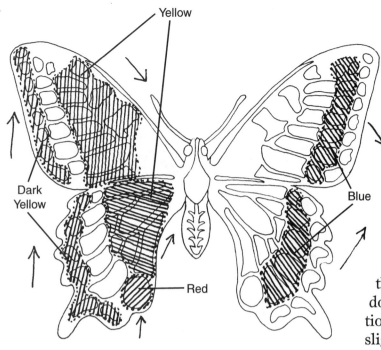

Yellow

Dark
Yellow

Blue

Red

2 *The arrow closest to the shaded section indicates the highlight direction (not the direction of the lines in the shading). The same color and highlight direction should be used on the corresponding section on the other wing.*

color blocks but *do not remove* the HeatnBond paper. Place the color blocks together, but do not overlap the fabric. Lay the black wing outline over the blocks to check the placement of the color. Trim the color blocks as needed.

Assembling the Banner

Construct the background fabric and iron it. Place a large sheet of used HeatnBond paper shiny side up on the work surface. Lay the color blocks in position with the HeatnBond paper side down. Remove the HeatnBond paper from the black outline fabric. Carefully lay the outline over the color blocks. Maneuver the color blocks under the outline fabric. Do not overlap the color blocks. As each piece is maneuvered into place, tack the black outline to it in several places. Then move on to the next color block. The used HeatnBond paper under the color blocks prevents the HeatnBond paper

attached to the color blocks from sticking to the work surface.

Once the black outline has been tacked to each colored block, carefully iron the outline to adhere it to the colored blocks.

Lift the butterfly from the used HeatnBond paper. Remove the HeatnBond paper from the color blocks. Lay the butterfly in position on the background fabric. Place a sheet of used HeatnBond paper over the butterfly. Iron the butterfly to the background fabric. You do not need to iron inside every cutout section of the wings. Instead, let the colors slightly puff through the holes to add to the lacing effect that makes this technique attractive. Make sure all the edges and the thin antennae are secured.

Finally, iron on the body parts, the eyes, and the wing supports (see diagram 3).

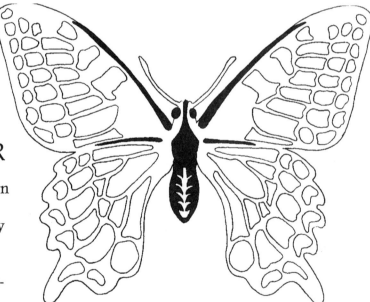

3 *The wing supports, eyes, and body parts are adhered last.*

We have let our light shine before people so that they will have seen our deeds and praise our Father in heaven.

SINCE 1954

Suggested Fabric and Colors

- Use white cotton for the background of the banner.
- For the outline fabric, use black cotton-poly broadcloth.
- For the eight rays, use satin. Consider a soft yellow in plain, mottled, print, and moiré fabrics. These fabrics and patterns will correspond in position to the patterns and fabrics used inside the globe.
- For the sections inside the globe that surround the flame, use off-white satin in plain, mottled, print, and moiré fabrics.
- The flame (from the center outward) should be silver, gold, and copper metallic lamés.
- The Bible page edges should be either red silk or red satin. The Bible pages should be bright white heavy satin (or this fabric may need to be lined so the black outline doesn't show through). For the Bible cover, use two shades of brown. The lighter fabric should be a cotton-poly blend. The darker fabric could be a suede-like fabric. Use this darker fabric on the thin "edge" of the cover that shows on the left side of the design.
- The fuel reservoir should be gold lamé. The highlights on the reservoir and the globe should be silver lamé.
- Make the letters from a complementary color. The letter *W* and the "since YEAR" could be done in a bright lamé on a black outline.

Special Notes for Making the Design Elements

Because of the complexity of the design, it is essential that you trace the design elements precisely. Remember to trace the same "side" of the line to ensure the pieces of fabric join together without gaps or overlap (see diagram 1).

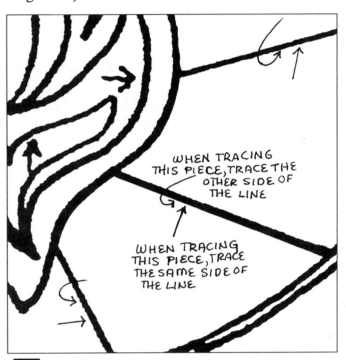

1 *Trace the same "side" of the line.*

When preparing the patterns for the eight rays outside the globe, add 1″ to the length of each pattern piece. Because the pieces must butt up to each other, the extra length will allow you to adjust the "fit" of the rays to fix any gaps. Note that the ray under the lamp and Bible goes all the way to the globe on either side of the lamp reservoir.

Add a little extra length to each section inside the globe as you prepare these pattern pieces. This will ensure that the flame will cover the ends of the sections when completed.

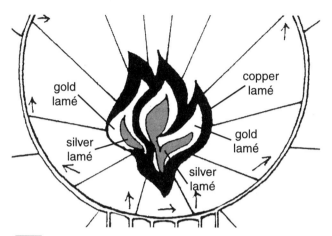

2 *The flame is five separate pieces.*

The flame is made from five separate pieces (see diagram 2). The bottom layer is copper lamé. The second layer is gold metallic lamé. And the third layer is silver lamé.

Do not outline the individual letters of the phrase. To construct the letter *W* and the "since YEAR," trace the letters and bond them to the black outline fabric. Then trace the letters again, only ⅛″ to ¼″ smaller. Bond these patterns to the decorative fabric.

ASSEMBLING THE BANNER

Place the rays in position on the background fabric. Adjust the rays so each edge butts up against the edge of the next piece. Tack the rays in position. When the rays are in place, iron them securely to the background.

Place the black outline in position and iron it down. Check the edges for adherence. The outline fabric should overlap the ends of the rays under the globe.

Place the design elements in position for the globe rays and highlights and the flame. Check for fit. Make sure the flame covers the edges of the sections inside the globe. Make adjustments as necessary, then tack the pieces in place. Continue down the reservoir, tacking each design element in place. Once the entire globe and reservoir is constructed, lay a sheet of used HeatnBond paper shiny side down over the design elements and bond them to the outline fabric.

Position the elements of the Bible. Check for fit and correct design elements as necessary. If you used silk, remove those pieces. Bond the heavier fabrics in place, then reposition the silk page edges, lower the iron temperature, and adhere the silk pieces.

Finally, position the letters and tack them in place. Let your eye correct the letter and word spacing. You will bond the outline fabric of the *W* and the "since YEAR" with the rest of the letters. Then bond the decorative fabric *W* and "since YEAR" to the outline fabric.

BAPTISM BANNER 1:
THE LAMB

Suggested Fabric and Colors

- Use light blue cotton for the background of the banner.
- For the sun, use bright light yellow satin for the circle. Use a combination of satin, moiré, and silkie fabrics in medium to light yellow for the rays of the sun.
- Use bright red, bright yellow, and bright royal blue satin or moiré for the rainbow. (Use heavy satins or moirés so the background fabric will not show through.)
- Use emerald green cotton for the grass.
- Use hunter green satin for the flower stems. Use satins in purple, pink, white, etc., for the flower petals and bright yellow satin for the flower centers.
- Use tan or brown cotton for the land between the grass and the water.
- Use black cotton-poly broadcloth for the lamb outline. Use a printed white silkie for the lamb's body and light tan cotton for the hooves.
- Use three colors of blue lamé or satin for the water. Use the same color for each arrow that points in the same direction.

Special Notes for Making the Design Elements

Make sure you number each pattern piece and write the number on the corresponding section of an intact photocopy of the design. There are numerous look-alike pieces, especially the flower petals. It might be helpful to put the petals for each flower in a separate plastic bag.

Assembling the Banner

Place the water sections on the background fabric. Tack them in place and iron them securely. Next, position the brown and green fabrics. Adhere them and check for secure edges.

Position the flower stems and tack them in place, but don't iron them down. Place the lamb outline in position, moving the stems as needed. Adhere the lamb outline and the stems on the right side of the lamb. Adhere the white fabric on top of the black outline. Place the stems of the flowers on the left side between the lamb's front legs and iron in position. Adhere the flower petals and centers.

Finally, position the sun, the sun's rays, and the rainbow pieces. Securely iron these elements in place. Check the entire banner for secure edges and re-iron as necessary.

Special Notes

You can make this banner for display during each baptism. You can add the top triangle and personal banner as show to the left of the banner design.

To construct the triangle, make an equilateral triangle from wood. The length of the sides should be the same as the width of the completed banner. Construct the baptismal shell banner as described on page 16. Stretch the finished design over the wooden triangle and staple it in place. To construct the personal baptismal banner, see the pattern on page 88. You can use the same background fabric for all three banners. Or use a white cotton for the background of the personal banner.

Screw cup hooks into the bottom of the wood triangle and attach them to the bottom of the personal banner. Then attach screw eyes to the top of the personal banner and the top of the lamb banner. Connect these to display the separate banners as one unit.

Baptism Banner 2:
Cross, Dove, and Shell

Suggested Fabric and Colors

- Use light blue cotton for the background of the banner.

- Use royal blue cotton or cotton chintz for the outline under the cross, dove, and shell.

- Use bright red cotton or cotton chintz for the second outline around the cross.

- Use gold lamé or another directional gold metallic fabric (one that is ribbed) for the cross.

- Make the dove from a pure white satin-like fabric, which could be slightly textured, mottled, or ribbed. Do not use a silkie. Make the beak from gold lamé.

- Use a directional silver fabric for the shell.

- Make the water droplets from medium blue cotton with light blue lamé highlights.

Special Notes for Making the Design Elements

Because you will be combining the shell design on page 16 with the dove design on page 36, review the specific directions for constructing these portions of the banner. Determine which highlight scheme you will follow for the shell and note it on the pattern for this banner. Also draw the arrows for the highlight scheme of the dove as shown on page 36 on this pattern. Remember to number each design element and the corresponding section of an intact photocopy of the design.

To construct the dove's head, trace the head and beak shape and bond the pattern to the same royal blue fabric used for the larger outline. Trace the head shape again, only $\frac{1}{8}''$ to $\frac{1}{4}''$ smaller. Bond the pattern to the white satin. Trace the beak shape again, only $\frac{1}{8}''$ to $\frac{1}{4}''$ smaller, and bond this pattern to the gold lamé.

To make the water droplets, trace the water droplets and bond them to the same royal blue fabric as the larger outline. Then trace the droplet shapes again, only $\frac{1}{8}''$ to $\frac{1}{4}''$ smaller. Bond these pattern pieces to the medium blue fabric.

Assembling the Banner

Place the royal blue outline in position on the background fabric and iron it in place. Position the red outline. Check for fit, then iron it and check for adherence. Position the gold cross and iron it securely.

Position the individual feathers and body sections of the dove. Check for fit, then tack the pieces in place. Place a used sheet of HeatnBond paper shiny side down over the dove. Firmly iron the dove in place. Check the edges for adherence. Place the outline of the dove's head in position. Bond it to the body. Then position the white head and bond it in place. Finally position the beak and bond it in place.

Place the shell sections in position and check for fit. Make adjustments as necessary and tack the pieces in place. Securely iron the shell using a used sheet of HeatnBond paper.

Finally, adhere the water droplets. First, bond the outline fabric. Then adhere the medium blue fabric. Finally, bond the blue lamé highlights.

CHRISTMAS BANNER

Today a Savior is born to you; He is Christ the Lord!

Suggested Fabric and Colors

- Use white cotton for the background of the banner.
- Use black cotton for the outline.
- The flowers can be made from a bright red suede-like (directional) fabric. The flower centers can be bright yellow cotton. The stems that connect the centers of the flowers should be yellow-green cotton.
- Make the leaves with more than one vein (there are eight) from green moiré.
- Use white satin for the candles.
- The flames should be silver lamé with gold lamé centers.
- The letters should be made from burgundy cotton. The letter *T* should be made from gold lamé on an outline of burgundy cotton.

Special Notes for Making the Design Elements

When tracing the outline shape, note that the areas in the design with heavy lines are sections that need to be cut out from the outline shape. The background fabric will show through these cutouts. It would be best to use an X-Acto knife to cut out the smaller sections.

The top layer of petals (those closest to the centers of the flowers) should be made from the bright red suede-like fabric. The second layer of petals should be made from red satin. The highlight direction of the petals and the leaves is determined by the vein. The veins in the petals are cutout sections.

Do not outline the individual letters. To construct the letter *T*, trace the shape and bond it to the burgundy cotton. Then trace the shape again, only ⅛″ to ¼″ smaller. Bond this pattern to the gold lamé.

Assembling the Banner

Position the outline shape on the background fabric and adhere it. Check for secure edges. Place the individual design elements in place and check for fit. Make any corrections and tack the pieces in place. Position a used sheet of HeatnBond paper over the design and iron the pieces firmly in place.

Finally, position the burgundy outline for the letter *T* in position. Lay the other letters in place around the *T.* Allow your eye to correct letter and word spacing. Bond the letters in place. Then bond the gold *T* in place on its burgundy outline.

Take eat, this is My body
Take drink, this is My blood . . . .
shed for you for the remisssion of sins . . . .

Suggested Fabric and Colors

- Use deep royal purple cotton for the background.

- For the outline, use black cotton.

- Make the fabric that drapes above and between the hands from medium to light purple satin. The sleeves and garment that are below the section that drapes should be medium purple satin. Make the sections inside the sleeves from satin that matches the color of the background fabric.

- Make the hands from either pale violet or flesh-toned suede-like fabric. The nail imprints could be deep violet or burgundy cotton.

- Make the bread crust from brown cotton and the center of the bread from off-white cotton with a tone-on-tone print.

- For the wheat kernels, use two different values of the same color of gold satin (one light, one medium). The wheat stem and leaves should be two different values of brown or tan. Use the darker of the two fabrics for the small portion of the leaf closest to the chalice and farthest from the bread.

- Make the grape leaf from green moiré. Use the same medium to light purple for the grapes as you use for the draping of the robe. The stem should be brown cotton.

- Use copper metallic for the interior of the chalice. Use silver metallic for the outside of the chalice.

- Use a nondirectional but highly reflective gold or silver fabric for the letters.

Special Notes for Making the Design Elements

You could use the lacing technique to construct the grapes. You also might try this technique with the heads of wheat.

Because of the numerous pieces (especially the wheat kernels and the grapes), it is essential that you number the individual pattern pieces and the corresponding sections on an intact photocopy of the design.

Do not outline the letters.

Assembling the Banner

Place the outline shape in position on the background fabric and adhere it securely. Carefully position the separate elements of the robe. Check for fit and correct any flaws. Tack in place as each piece is moved into position. Follow the same procedure to place the rest of the design elements. Once all the elements are in place, lay a used sheet of HeatnBond paper shiny side down over the fabric and firmly iron the pieces in place.

CONFIRMATION BANNER

Suggested Fabric and Colors

- Use red cotton for the background of the banner.
- The outline fabric should be a black cotton-poly blend.
- Use a brown suede-like fabric for the cross.
- The rays in the circle around the cross and the nimbus could be made from gold lamé. Or make the rays in primary colors.
- Use heavy white satin that is ribbed or visually textured for the dove. Use gold lamé for the beak.
- Make the Bible pages from heavy white satin. The Bible cover can be the same brown suede-like fabric as the cross. The page edges could be gold lamé.
- The portion of the bookmark that lays across the top of the Bible could be made from bright red silk. The small section to the left of the bookmark at the top of the Bible should be burgundy silk. The portion of the bookmark that drops from the Bible should be a slightly deeper red silk or satin.
- Use a complementary fabric for the letters. They could be outlined, depending on the fabric you choose for the letters.

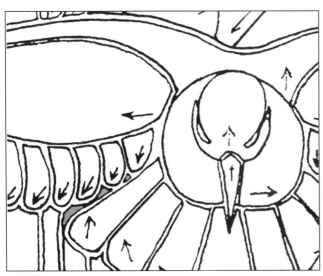

1 *The shaded areas are cutout sections.*

Special Notes for Making the Design Elements

As you trace the outline shape, note that there are two small cutouts under the dove's wing, above the tail, and to the right of the cross (see diagram 1). The red background fabric will show through these cutouts.

The gap between the nimbus and the circle of rays is also the red background fabric showing between the design elements. There is no black outline behind the nimbus or the rays.

It is essential that you number the individual design elements and the corresponding section on an intact photocopy of the design. Pay careful attention to the highlight direction on the separate sections of the dove and on the different rays.

To construct the dove's head, trace the head and beak shape and bond it to the same fabric used for the larger outline. Trace the head shape again, only ⅛" to ¼" smaller. Bond it to the white satin. Trace the beak shape again, only ⅛" to ¼" smaller, and bond it to the gold lamé.

Assembling the Banner

Position the outline fabric and bond it in place on the background fabric. Position the rays and the sections of the nimbus. Make sure there is a uniform "border" of red showing between the ends of the rays and the nimbus sections. Bond the pieces in position. Bond the elements of the Bible in place.

Position the individual design elements of the dove, check for fit, and bond in place. Position the outline of the dove's head and bond in place. Then position the white dove's head and bond it to the outline. Finally, bond the beak in position.

Bond the letters in place, allowing your eye to adjust letter and word spacing.

Easter Banner 1: Crown and Butterfly

HIS VICTORY IS OURS

SUGGESTED FABRIC AND COLORS

- Use a soft butter yellow for the background of the banner.
- Use black cotton for the outline fabric.
- Make the "front" of the crown from gold lamé. The shaded "inside" of the crown should be copper lamé (see diagram 1).

2 *The shaded areas are cutout sections.*

(See diagram 2 if you are unsure what needs to be cut out.) The yellow background fabric will show through these cutouts. Use an X-Acto knife to cut out these smaller sections.

The fabric and color choices for this butterfly are different than the sampler design. You can use either color scheme. You will want to transfer the highlight direction scheme from the sampler design to this one. Follow the directions on the sampler to prepare the butterfly for bonding to the background fabric.

The direction of the "vein" in the petals of the lilies will determine the highlight direction. Follow the "line" of the individual stems and leaves to determine the highlight direction for these pieces.

Make sure to number each design piece and the corresponding section on an intact photocopy of the design.

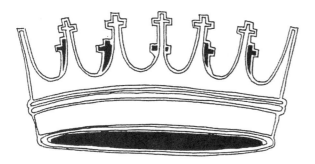

1 *The shaded areas are the "inside" of the crown.*

- The butterfly outline is black cotton. The color blocks for the wings should be a brilliant yellow silkie with a tone-on-tone print and a brilliant royal blue directional metallic fabric.
- For the lilies, use an off-white and a bright white ribbed satin-like fabric (these fabrics may need to be lined). The bulbs of the lilies should be light pale green satin. Make the leaves from three different shades of green satin.
- The letters can be made from a complementary color. They could be outlined.

SPECIAL NOTES FOR MAKING THE DESIGN ELEMENTS

You will trace individual outlines for each section of the banner. Note that the areas in the lilies with heavy lines are sections that need to be cut out from the outline fabric.

ASSEMBLING THE BANNER

Construct the butterfly following the directions on page 22. Then place the outline for the crown, the butterfly, the outline for the lilies, and the letters in position. Adjust as necessary for a pleasing presentation. Allow your eye to adjust the "white" space surrounding each separate element. Use pins to mark positions for these elements.

Remove the butterfly, the lily outline, and the letters. Bond the crown outline in position. Then bond the rest of the crown design elements in place. Next, bond the butterfly in position, referring to your pins. Then build the lilies. Finally, bond the letters in position.

EASTER BANNER 2: CROSS AND LILY

SUGGESTED FABRIC AND COLORS

- Use white cotton for the background of the banner.
- Use black cotton for the outline fabric.
- Make the cross from gold lamé or another directional gold fabric.
- Make the lily bulbs from light pale green cotton. The leaves and stems should be green satin. The open lily petals should be a bright white ribbed satin-like fabric (this fabric may need to be lined).

ASSEMBLING THE BANNER

Place the outline fabric in position on the background fabric. Adhere it securely to the background fabric. Position the separate design elements, check for fit, and tack in place. Finally, lay a used sheet of HeatnBond paper over the design and securely adhere the design elements.

Suggested Fabric and Colors

- Use white cotton for the background of the banner.
- Use black cotton for the outline fabric.
- Make the trumpets from gold lamé, copper lamé, and silver lamé. The inside of the trumpet will be copper with gold fabric forming the highlight (the two pieces that form the "trumpet" shape inside the rim). The center section of each horn stem is the silver highlight on top of the gold fabric. Make the rim of the trumpets gold.
- The lily bulbs should be made from pale green satin. The "vein" of the bulbs should be a light green satin. Use the same fabric for the bulbs of the open lilies. The petals of the open lilies should be made from a bright white ribbed satin-like fabric. The underbelly of the petals should be made from an off-white ribbed satin-like fabric. Use bright yellow cotton for the centers of the lilies. Use bright, medium, and dark green satin for the stems and leaves.
- Make the letters from a nondirectional gold or silver metallic fabric. Use black cotton to outline all the letters or only the word *alleluia*.

Special Notes for Making the Design Elements

Pay careful attention when tracing and cutting out the outline fabric. There are numerous cutout sections. The black areas of the pattern identify these cutouts. Use an X-Acto knife for the smaller cutouts.

Because of the numerous pieces, it is essential that you number every design element and the corresponding section of an intact photocopy of the design. You might place the pieces of each flower and trumpet in a separate plastic bag to avoid confusing the design elements.

Pay careful attention to matching the highlight direction. In general, the highlight will match the "vein" of the petals or the "slope" of the individual leaves and stems.

When making the trumpets, the copper section inside the bell will be an oval shape. The gold highlight pieces will be ironed on top of this piece. The gold "stem" of the trumpets will be on top of the black outline fabric. The silver highlight that runs down the center of the trumpets will be ironed on top of the gold fabric.

To outline the letters, first trace the shapes and bond them to the black fabric. Then trace the letters again, only ⅛″ to ¼″ smaller. Bond these to the decorative fabric.

Assembling the Banner

Place the outline fabric in position on the background fabric and iron it securely. First, place the flowers and bulbs in position. Adjust the fit and tack these in place. Then add the trumpet pieces. Adjust the fit and tack in place. Finally, add the stems and leaves. Adjust the fit and tack in place. Check the overall presentation of the banner and make any adjustments to the fit of the design elements. Then place a sheet of used HeatnBond paper over the design and firmly adhere the pieces.

Position the outlines for the individual letters. Allow your eye to adjust the letter and word spacing. Bond the outlines in place. Then bond the decorative fabric letters to the outline fabric.

FUNERAL BANNER

SUGGESTED FABRIC AND COLORS

- The background of the banner should be white cotton.

- Use dark forest green cotton for the outline of the flower, leaves, and the stem.

- Use black cotton for the outline of the butterfly, which includes the antennae.

- For the color blocks of the butterfly's wings, use a bright royal blue metallic, a bright yellow silkie with a tone-on-tone print, and a bright red-orange silkie. Make the wing supports from gray cotton. Use dark brown cotton for the body. Use metallic green fabric for the eyes.

- Use two shades of green satin for the leaves. Place the darker shade on the upper portion of each leaf.

- The flower petals are constructed in layers. The layer bonded to the outline fabric on all three petals should be pale light green cotton. The next layer should be a brilliant white ribbed satin-like fabric (this fabric may need to be lined). This white fabric is cut out in the vein pattern to reveal the pale green below (see diagram 1).

- The center of the flower petal immediately above the head of the butterfly is also constructed in layers. The layer bonded to the light green fabric should be a yellow-orange silkie. Use bright yellow satin to make the stamen, which are bonded to the yellow-orange silkie (see diagram 2).

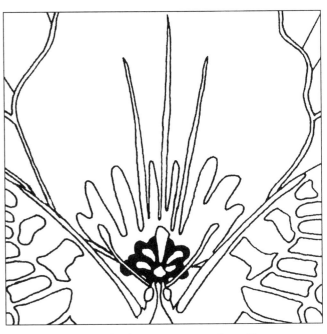

2 *The dark shading represents the yellow-orange center. The white areas represent the stamen.*

- The flower stem should be made from the same dark green satin used for the leaves.

- For the rays in the background, use a pastel color theme in blues, pinks, and yellows. Find a wide variety of fabrics in these colors. Include broad and narrow moirés, satin iridescent lamés, and silkies. Use the same fabric for each letter in the design.

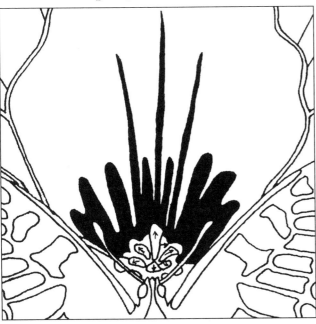

1 *The shaded areas are cut out to reveal the pale green fabric.*

SPECIAL NOTES FOR MAKING THE DESIGN ELEMENTS

Follow the instructions on page 22 to construct the butterfly. Set the finished butterfly aside until you have assembled the rays and the flower.

Pay careful attention to highlight direction. Number all the separate design elements and the corresponding sections on an intact photocopy of the design.

Lay the individual pieces in place and check for fit before bonding any elements to the background or outline fabrics. Make any corrections to the separate elements and re-trace and re-cut pieces as necessary.

Make the rays that form the background at least ½″ longer on both ends. This will help you match the edges. It also will ensure that the flower and butterfly will cover the ends of the rays in the center of the banner.

When tracing the green outline fabric, keep in mind that it extends below the butterfly. Just connect the lines the butterfly covers. When assembling the banner, double-check that the butterfly fits over the outline shape.

To make the variegated highlight pattern in the petals, lay the fabric right side down on the work surface. Pull the selvage edge at regular intervals, keeping the fabric flat. This will cause the highlight to ripple across the petal. Place the HeatnBond paper on the fabric and gently iron in place to make a permanent visual "ripple" (see diagram 3).

Make this banner for permanent display at your church. Construct the smaller personal banner on page 89 for display at the funeral service. Then give the personal banner to the family.

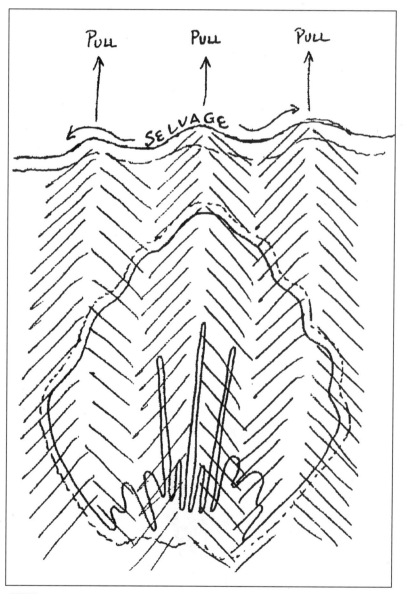

3 *To make the highlight pattern, gently pull the fabric, then bond it to the paper.*

ASSEMBLING THE BANNER

Lay all the pieces in place on the background fabric and check for fit. Then remove the top layers. Position the dark green outline and lay the first of the 45 rays in place to the left of the stem. Continue placing the rays clockwise around the outline. When all the rays are in position, check that the edges butt up against each other (but don't overlap) and that the ends of the rays overlap the green outline. Lightly tack the rays as you fit them together.

After all the rays are correctly positioned and tacked in place, gently remove the outline fabric. Bond the rays along the outer edge of the banner, section by section. Re-align the ends of the rays that will be under the outline fabric. Carefully bond the inner portion of the rays, section by section.

To build the rest of the banner, begin by adhering the dark green outline fabric over the rays. Then lay the completed butterfly on the flower outline to accurately position the rest of the design elements. First, place the light pale green sections on the outline fabric. Lay the rest of the flower pieces in position on the pale green fabric. Add the leaves and stem. Make sure the leaves, stem, and petals butt up against the butterfly. Tack all the flower pieces in position. Remove the butterfly. Adhere the design elements of the flower. Replace the butterfly and adhere it to the banner.

INDEPENDENCE DAY: UNITED STATES

We are thankful for those who gave their lives to win our country's freedom. We give thanks and praise to Jesus for the life He gave to win our eternal freedom!

SUGGESTED FABRIC AND COLORS

- Make the background of the banner from light blue cotton.
- The outline fabric should be black cotton.
- The nails that form the interior of the cross should be silver lamé. Use gray cotton for the shadows in the cross (see diagram 1).

1 *The shaded sections indicate the shadows in the cross.*

- The rays should be made from a moiré, a satin, and a silkie that are the same color as the background fabric. The moiré fabric will be used for the wide rays. Alternate the silkie and the satin for the narrow rays.
- Use navy blue for the field behind the stars. Make the stars from white satin (this fabric may need to be lined).
- Make the pole and ring from gray cotton.
- Make the stripes from bright red and bright white satin (the top stripe is red). Also make the left edge of the flag from white satin.

- Make the letters from a coordinating solid fabric. They do not need to be outlined.

SPECIAL NOTES FOR MAKING THE DESIGN ELEMENTS

Make sure that you number the individual design elements and the corresponding sections on an intact photocopy of the design. You might want to place all the stars in a plastic bag so they do not get lost.

Pay careful attention to the highlight direction, especially on the stripes. The highlight in the stars will follow the direction of the top point.

When making the patterns for the rays, add 1″ to the length. This will ensure that the rays extend under the cross and that the edges butt up against each other. Where the cross or flag cut into a ray, the ray is a continuous piece of fabric and the cross or flag fabric is bonded on top of the ray.

ASSEMBLING THE BANNER

Position the rays and lay the outline of the cross in place on the background fabric. Check that the rays butt up against each other but do not overlap. Tack the rays in position. Then position the flag pieces (except the stars). Make sure the rays butt up against the flag. Tack the flag pieces in position. Remove the black cross outline. Adhere the rays and the flag pieces.

Reposition the cross outline and adhere it to the banner. Adhere the nails and shadows. Position the stars and tack in place. Adhere these elements.

Finally, place the letters on the banner. Allow your eye to adjust the spacing between letters and words. Adhere the letters.

INDEPENDENCE DAY: CANADA

We are thankful for those who gave their lives to win our country's freedom. We give thanks and praise to Jesus for the life He gave to win our eternal freedom!

Suggested Fabric and Colors

- Make the background of the banner from light blue cotton.

- The outline fabric should be black cotton.

- The nails that form the interior of the cross should be silver lamé. Use gray cotton for the shadows in the cross (see diagram 1).

1 *The shaded sections indicate the shadows in the cross.*

- The rays should be made from a moiré, a satin, and a silkie that are the same color as the background fabric. The moiré fabric will be used for the wide rays. Alternate the silkie and the satin for the narrow rays.

- Make the center section of the flag from white satin (this fabric may need to be lined). Use orange satin for the two side sections of the flag and for the maple leaf. The curled part of the flag should be made from light orange satin.

Special Notes for Making the Design Elements

Make sure that you number the individual design elements and the corresponding sections on an intact photocopy of the design.

Pay careful attention to the highlight direction, especially on the rays.

When making the patterns for the rays, add 1″ to the length. This will ensure that the rays extend under the cross and that the edges butt up against each other. Where the cross or flag cut into a ray, the ray is a continuous piece of fabric and the cross or flag fabric is bonded on top of the ray.

Assembling the Banner

Position the rays and lay the outline of the cross in place on the background fabric. Check that the rays butt up against each other but do not overlap. Tack the rays in position. Then position the flag pieces. Make sure the rays butt up against the flag. Tack the flag pieces in position. Remove the black cross outline. Adhere the rays and the flag pieces.

Reposition the cross outline and adhere it to the banner. Adhere the nails and shadows.

Finally, place the letters on the banner. Allow your eye to adjust the spacing between letters and words. Adhere the letters.

THE MISSION FIELD

GO AND TELL

... for it is not you speaking but the Spirit of the Father speaking through you.

Suggested Fabric and Colors

This banner design includes four smaller designs that surround the cross. The fabric and color directions for these smaller sections appear separately.

- Use butter yellow, light blue, or white cotton for the background of the banner.
- Use black cotton for the outline fabric. *Note:* There are two layers on the cross, both of which are outlined by black.
- The outer layer of the cross should be gold lamé. Use white moiré for the top layer of the cross.
- Make the heart from a red metallic fabric.
- The letters on the cross should be black cotton chintz with no outline fabric.
- Each of the four designs is bonded on a gold lamé square, which frames it.
- Make the letters for "Go and Tell" from a calico cotton print bonded to a black cotton outline.
- The rest of the letters should be made from a solid fabric that coordinates with the calico or from black cotton.

Special Notes for Making the Design Elements

Make sure you number each piece and write the number in the corresponding section of an intact photocopy of the design. You might want to place all the pieces for each square in a plastic bag.

To construct the outlined letters, trace the letters and bond them to the black outline fabric. Then trace the letters again, only ⅛″ to ¼″ smaller. Bond these patterns to the calico fabric.

For the water sections in the cityscape and the country scene, all the vertical arrows should be the lightest shade of blue. All the horizontal arrows should be the darkest shade. And all the rest of the sections should be the medium shade.

Use an X-Acto knife to cut out the windows in the farmhouse.

Suggested Fabric and Colors for the Cityscape

- Use black cotton for the outline fabric. This piece is actually a square to which the separate design elements will be adhered.
- Use three shades of blue metallic (light, medium, and dark) for the water.
- Use brown cotton for the section between the water and the buildings.
- Make the first row of buildings from chocolate brown cotton. Make the second row from medium rust-brown cotton. Make the third row from orange-brown or deep orange cotton. (Don't use bright orange.)
- From top to bottom, make the sections of the sky light blue satin (which matches the light blue water section), pale orange satin, yellow-orange satin, deep yellow satin, and light yellow satin (this color is behind the buildings).

Suggested Fabric and Colors for the Country Scene

- Use black cotton for the outline fabric. This piece is actually a square to which the separate design elements will be adhered.
- Use sky blue heavy cotton (or line a lightweight cotton) for the sky.
- Make the sun, including the rays, from gold lamé.
- Use three shades of green satin for the hills. Make the farthest hill the lightest shade. The middle hill and the grass section under the farm buildings should be the medium shade. Use the brightest, deepest shade for the section under the sheep.
- Use hunter green cotton for the tree and bush.
- Make the rocks from light gray cotton.

- Use a white silkie with a tone-on-tone print for the sheep.
- For the buildings, use red cotton for the roof of the house and gray cotton for the roof of the barn and silo. Make the walls of the barn and silo from rust-red cotton. The walls of the house should be white cotton (this fabric may need to be lined). The windows are cutouts that reveal the black outline fabric.

SUGGESTED FABRIC AND COLORS FOR THE HOUSE

- Use black cotton for the outline fabric. This piece is actually a square to which the separate design elements will be adhered.
- Use the same blue for the sky that you used for the country scene.
- Make the house from white cotton (this fabric may need to be lined). The shutters should be made from burgundy or red cotton. The window frames should be brown cotton. The windowpanes and the window in the door should be soft yellow cotton. The door should be red cotton. Make the roof from three shades of red: All the number 1s should be medium red cotton. All the number 2s should be pale rust-red cotton. All the number 3s should be burgundy cotton. Make the chimney from the same white cotton as the house. The chimney top can be either white or the same medium red used on the roof.
- The bushes should be hunter green cotton or satin.
- Use light gray cotton for the step. The riser (front) of the step should be medium gray cotton. Make the stone sidewalk the same light gray cotton as the step.
- The grass should be green satin or cotton.
- Make the fence from the same white cotton as the house.

SUGGESTED FABRIC AND COLORS FOR THE GLOBE

- Use a dark blue cotton for the outline fabric. This piece is actually a square to which the separate design elements will be adhered.
- Use medium blue cotton for the outer ring and light blue satin for the inner ring. (The centers of both rings will be cut out to reveal the dark blue outline fabric.)
- Use light green cotton for the continents and islands.
- Use royal blue satin for the oceans.

ASSEMBLING THE BANNER

Carefully position the separate design pieces on the background fabric and check for fit. Then remove the design elements.

Position the first black outline of the cross (the smaller of the two outlines). Also position the gold lamé outlines for the four sections. Adhere these to the background fabric. Then adhere the separate layers of the cross. (Layer 2 is the gold lamé, layer 3 is the next black outline, and layer 4 is the white moiré.)

Adhere the background of the cityscape to the banner. Beginning at the bottom, position the water sections and check for fit. Try to leave a uniform border of black around the sections. Tack in place. Position the brown section and tack in place. Then position the building sections and tack in place. Finally place the sky sections and tack in position. Lay a sheet of used HeatnBond paper over the square and adhere all the design elements.

Adhere the background fabric of the house to the banner. Position the sky and grass sections and tack in place. Then position the elements of the house and roof and tack in place. Place the bushes, the steps, the stone walkway, and the fenceposts and tack in place. Check for fit. Then place a sheet of used HeatnBond paper over the design elements and adhere them to the banner.

Adhere the country scene background to the banner. Starting at the top, position the sky, sun, and hill sections. Tack in place. Then position the water sections and the rocks and tack in place. Add the sheep, tree, bush, and farm buildings and tack in place. Check for fit and make corrections as necessary. Then place a sheet of used HeatnBond paper over the design elements and adhere them to the banner.

Adhere the background of the globe to the banner. Position the rings, the land masses, and the water. Check for fit. Make sure the outline is uniform around the land and water sections. Place a sheet of used HeatnBond

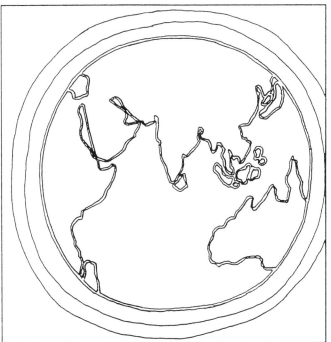

paper over the design elements and adhere them to the banner.

Once the four squares have been bonded to the banner background, position the heart and bond it in place. Then adhere the words to the cross. Finally, position the words at the bottom of the banner. Allow your eye to adjust the spacing between the letters and words. Bond the black outline of "Go and Tell" first, then adhere the calico letters.

IF MY PEOPLE, WHO ARE CALLED BY MY NAME, WILL HUMBLE THEMSELVES AND PRAY SEEK MY FACE AND TURN FROM THEIR WICKED WAYS, THEN WILL I HEAR FROM HEAVEN FORGIVE THEIR SIN AND HEAL THEIR LAND.

Suggested Fabric and Colors

- Make the background of the banner from white cotton.
- Use black cotton chintz for the outline fabric.
- The fabric behind the stars should be navy blue cotton.
- Make the stars from heavy white satin. Make the stripes from bright red satin and bright white satin (this fabric may need to be lined). The top stripe is red.
- Make the hands and arms from a flesh-tone suede-like fabric. The nail prints should be red cotton.
- Make the letters and the small cross from navy chintz.

Special Notes for Making the Design Elements

Make sure you number the individual pieces and write the number in the corresponding section on an intact photocopy of the design.

Pay careful attention to the highlights, especially in the stripes behind the hands and arms.

The black outline fabric extends beneath the entire center rectangle. Make this rectangle ⅛″ to ¼″ larger than the interior design so a small black outline will frame the design.

The lines in the arms are cutout sections of the flesh-tone fabric that reveal the black outline fabric beneath.

Assembling the Banner

Adhere the black rectangle in the center of the background fabric. Position the arm and hand pieces and check for fit. Tack in place. Then add the flag elements and tack in place. Check position and make corrections as necessary. Adhere the design elements.

Finally, position the letters around the outside of the banner. Allow your eye to adjust the spacing between the letters and the words. Adhere the letters and the cross.

National Day of Prayer: Canada

58

Suggested Fabric and Colors

- Make the background from white cotton.
- Use black cotton chintz for the outline fabric.
- The fabric behind the maple leaf should be white satin.
- Make the maple leaf from orange satin.
- Make the hands and arms from a flesh-tone suede-like fabric. The nail prints should be red cotton.
- Make the letters and the small cross from deep rust chintz.

Special Notes for Making the Design Elements

Make sure you number the individual pieces and write the number in the corresponding section on an intact photocopy of the design.

Pay careful attention to the highlights, especially in the separate elements of the flag.

The white satin that forms the flag should extend under the maple leaf.

The black outline fabric extends beneath the entire center rectangle. Make this rectangle $\frac{1}{8}''$ to $\frac{1}{4}''$ larger than the interior design so a small black outline will frame the design.

The lines in the arms are cutout sections of the flesh-tone fabric that reveal the black outline fabric beneath.

Assembling the Banner

Adhere the black rectangle in the center of the background fabric. Position the arm and hand pieces and check for fit. Tack in place. Then add the flag elements and tack in place. Check position and make corrections as necessary. Adhere the design elements.

Finally, position the letters around the outside of the banner. Allow your eye to adjust the spacing between the letters and the words. Adhere the letters and the cross.

ORDINATION BANNER

Suggested Fabric and Colors

- Use red cotton for the background of the banner.
- Make the outline from black cotton.
- Use gray cotton to make the cover of the Bible. The page edges should be gold lamé. The pages should be white satin (this fabric may need to be lined).
- Make the sword handle from a black suede-like fabric. One side of the sword blade should be gray cotton. The other side should be silver lamé.
- The inner part of the flame should be light yellow satin. The outer portion should be orange satin.
- Make the lamp from gold lamé. Use silver lamé for the highlights.
- Make the letters from black chintz.

Special Notes for Making the Design Elements

The edges of the sword blade that run into the lamp and the flame are cutout sections that reveal the black outline fabric.

There is a cutout section to the right of the largest flame. It reveals the red background fabric.

The highlights on the lamp should be adhered over the gold lamé.

Assembling the Banner

Position the outline fabric on the background fabric and adhere it. Position the rest of the design elements. Check for fit and tack in place. Lay a sheet of used HeatnBond paper over the design and adhere the elements to the banner.

PRAISE BANNER

Shout with joy
   to God,
    all the earth!
Sing the glory
  of His name;
  make His praise
   glorious!

Shout for joy to the LORD,
   all the earth.
Worship the LORD,
   with gladness;
come before Him with joyful songs.
Enter His gates with thanksgiving
  and His courts with praise;
 For the LORD is good and His Love
   endures forever!

Come, let us sing for
joy to the LORD; let
us shout aloud to the
Rock of our salvation.
Let us come before Him
with thanksgiving and
extol Him with music
  and song.

Clap your hands,
all you nations;
  shout to God
  with cries of joy.
  How awesome
is the LORD Most High,
  the great King
over all the earth!

Sing to the LORD a new
song; sing to the
LORD, all the earth. Sing
to the LORD, praise His
name; proclaim His
salvation day after day.

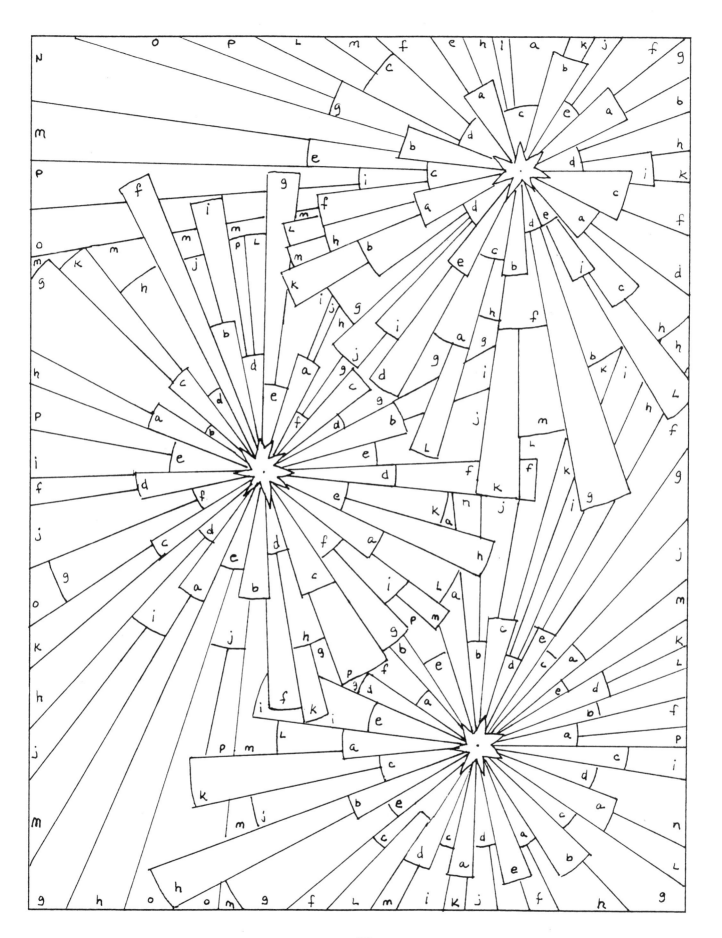

Suggested Fabric and Colors

The fabric store is your paint pallet for this banner. You can use virtually every type of fabric in almost every color under the sun. You will want to avoid lightweight silks, though, which would be difficult to bond to the background fabric without dimpling and ruining the fabric.

The color scheme can be done in two ways.

1. Use black cotton as the background fabric. Make the rays from brilliant, vibrant colors. When the rays are adhered to the background fabric, leave a narrow outline around each ray. Or you can use gold or silver lamé for the background fabric. (The lamé would need to be lined with a cotton for sturdiness.) Again, leave a narrow outline around each ray. Make the centers of each of the star bursts from gold or silver lamé. The center is placed over the ends of the rays. Make the letters from white cotton.

2. Construct a background fabric of gold or silver lamé lined with white cotton. Make the rays from pastel colors. Some of these fabrics may need to be lined. Each star burst can combine fabrics in pastel shades of a primary color. Or mix the pastel colors among the star bursts. Leave a narrow outline around each ray. The centers of the star bursts should be gold or silver lamé placed over the ends of the rays. Make the letters from black cotton or another dark color.

Special Notes for Making the Design Elements

If you are using option number 1, the "gaudier" the colors, the more brilliant the banner. Deep bright purples, reds, greens, yellows, and blues work well (but go easy on oranges). Be careful not to get too light or the white letters will not show up. Don't use fabrics that you can see through or that detract from the text.

If you are using option number 2, use few metallic fabrics. Place the palest colors in the center of the star bursts and move to more intense colors on the outer rays. Again, make sure the fabrics do not detract from the text.

When constructing the letters for the text, the letters should be from a solid fabric that coordinates with the banner colors (black or white are suggested, but another solid color may work too). Except for the initial letter, the letters should not be outlined. For the initial letter, use a printed metallic fabric adhered to an outline made from the same solid fabric as the other letters. To make the initial letter, trace the letter and bond it to the outline fabric. Then trace the letter again, only 1/8" to 1/4" smaller. Bond this to the decorative fabric.

Each ray is identified on the pattern with a letter. Those rays identified with the letters A-E should be the lightest colors (this applies to either color scheme). Those rays identified with the letters F-J should be corresponding colors in a medium shade. The rays identified with the letters K-P should be corresponding colors in the darkest or most vibrant shade.

When you assign fabrics to the letters, pay attention to what fabrics will be next to each other. Avoid putting two busy fabrics next to each other (for example, a damask and a moiré). Instead, put a satin or a solid silkie between the busy fabrics. Also keep in mind that moiré fabrics work best for the wide rays.

When making the patterns for the rays, add at least 1″ to the length of each ray on the outer edge. This will help you adjust the rays and ensure they are positioned correctly. (It's easier to cut away the extra length than to add a small piece of fabric to lengthen the ray.)

When you enlarge the pattern to make the banner, the lines will become thicker. Trace only the inside of the line for each ray. The width of the line will form the outline around each ray. The outline should be between ⅛″ and ¼″ wide.

You can determine your own highlight scheme for this banner. One option is to have the same highlight direction for each fabric. This helps conserve fabric, and if it's planned correctly, neighboring rays will not have the same highlight direction.

A 21′ × 8′ banner similar to this one required special accommodations to find a light source. To make a banner of this size, it's easier to trace each burst onto a separate tablecloth paper pattern, then put them together. Make sure you number every piece and write the number in the corresponding section on an intact photocopy of the design.

ASSEMBLING THE BANNER

To build the banner, measure to the center of each star burst and position the lamé centers. Tack in place.

Beginning from the outside edge, lay the rays in position one at a time. Make sure there is a relatively uniform outline between the individual rays. The lamé centers should overlap the ends of the rays at the center. Position all the rays for one star burst before moving on to the next. When each layer of rays is in position, tack them in place.

Once all the rays are in position, lay a sheet of used HeatnBond paper over the design. Bond the rays in small sections. Finally, bond the lamé centers over the ends of the rays.

Positioning of the words is important for the overall effect of this banner. Page 62 lists five possible psalm passages. These or any other verse of your choice would be appropriate for use on the banner. The three small banner samples at the top of page 62 give you some options for placing the text on the banner. To explore the placement of the text, make a transparency of the text you have chosen and move it across the surface of the banner design until you are satisfied. Then adhere the letters based on this positioning.

It takes a significant time commitment to construct this banner. However, when you have completed this project, it will make a dramatic statement in the church sanctuary.

Put on the full Armor of God

Then with Prayer Go onward Christian Soldiers!

Suggested Fabric and Colors

- Use black cotton for the background of the banner. If the background fabric is black, there will be no outline fabric. As you adhere the individual design elements, leave a gap between the pieces. If you use a different color for the background, then you will need to cut the outline shape from black cotton.

- Make the shield from heavy white satin that has a texture or make it from heavy white moiré. Make the cross from bright red silk or satin. Make the crown from a gold metallic fabric.

- Make the helmet from silver lamé. The ribs in the helmet (above the nose piece) and the bottom edge should carry the brightest highlight. The inside of the helmet should be medium gray cotton. The brush support (the section between the helmet and the brush) should be silver lamé. Make the large section above the brush support from medium red satin. The top of the brush should be light red-orange satin. The shadow areas at the front and the back of the brush should be burgundy satin.

- Make the sword handle from a leather-like brown fabric. The circle at the end of the handle should be silver lamé. Make the hand guard (the wide area with no arrows on either side of the handle) from medium gray cotton. The hand guard edge and the sword blade should be silver lamé.

- Make the belt from a brown leather-like fabric. The inside of the belt should be a dark leather-like fabric. The triangle should be a nondirectional gold metallic fabric. Make the dove from heavy white satin.

- Make the letters from heavy white cotton or another solid fabric that coordinates with the design elements and stands out from the background fabric. You may choose to outline all the letters or only the first letter.

Special Notes for Making the Design Elements

Note that the highlight arrows in the cross arms are vertical and parallel to the banner edge, not to the "tilt" of the cross on the shield.

The cross and crown shape should be cut from the white fabric so the background fabric can act as the outline. This means the cross arms do not extend below the crown. The same applies to the triangle and dove. This shape should be cut from the brown fabric so the background fabric can act as the outline. This means the triangle does not extend under the dove.

Assembling the Banner

Position the design elements on the background fabric, being careful to leave a uniform outline around the separate elements. Tack the pieces in place as each portion of the design is assembled. Then adhere the design elements, section by section.

Finally, position the letters. Allow your eye to adjust the spacing between the letters and words. Adhere the letters.

If you are using an outline fabric, you will adhere this fabric first, then build the banner on top of the outline.

SUNDAY SCHOOL BANNER

FEED MY LAMBS

There are four sections to this banner: the garment/body, the face, the hands, and the feet. The full-size design on page 68 should be used to construct the pattern for the garment/body and the text. Then use it to position the head, hands, and feet accurately. The designs for these other sections of the banner are on pages 70, 72, and 73. Make sure, however, that the size of the head, hands, and feet match the size of the full-size pattern.

Build this banner in stages to avoid confusing the different design elements.

SUGGESTED FABRIC AND COLORS

- Use butter yellow cotton for the background of the banner.
- Use light steel blue cotton for the outline fabric of the garment (right sleeve, upper body, right hip, left sleeve, and lower garment). Use burgundy cotton for the outline fabric of the sash and the area under the left arm.
- Use white satin for the garment and light burgundy satin for the sash (not an orange-red). The inside curl of the draped sash should be dark burgundy cotton (darker than the outline fabric). Make the belt from the same burgundy cotton used for the outline fabric for the sash. (See diagram 1 to identify the belt sections.)
- Use black cotton to outline letters made from light butter yellow cotton (or other complementary color). Do not make the letters from satin.

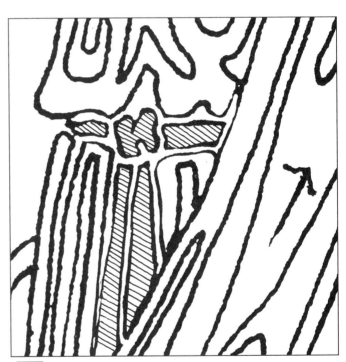

1 *The shaded sections form the belt.*

Fabric and color selections for the head, hands, and feet appear with the separate patterns.

Suggested Fabric and Colors for the Face

- Use dark brown cotton for the outline fabric.

- Make the beard/mustache and eyebrows from medium brown satin.

- Use three different shades of brown fabric for the hair. For those sections marked with an *A*, use medium brown satin; for those sections marked with a *B*, use dark brown satin; and for those sections marked with a *C*, use a dark brown suede-like fabric.

- Make the face and neck from a light medium to light brown suede-like fabric. Trace the face section as one piece (see diagram 2). Make the central forehead and nose section, the nostrils, the cheek-bones, the eye highlights (the small strips of fabric under and over the lids), the small triangular highlights on the inside corner of both eyes, and the highlight of the lower lip from a light brown suede-like fabric (see diagram 3).

- Make the teeth from off-white cotton.

- Make the interior of the nostrils from the same fabric you used for the outline.

- The eyes are layered as follows: off-white satin for the "whites" of the eyes; black cotton for the outer "ring" of the pupil (which extends under the iris); dark brown cotton for the inner circle of the pupil; and copper metallic fabric for the iris. Diagram 4 shows the pattern pieces for the parts of the eyes.

- For the mustache, cut a piece of dark brown cotton as defined by the dotted line and the bottom "edge" of the mustache (see diagram 5). You will place this under the medium brown satin used for the beard/mustache.

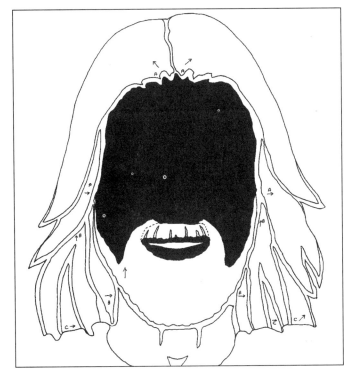

2 *The "shape" of the face section.*

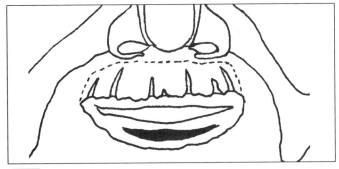

3 *The highlight of the lower lip.*

4 *The parts of the eye.*

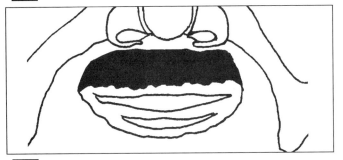

5 *You will need to outline the mustache area.*

71

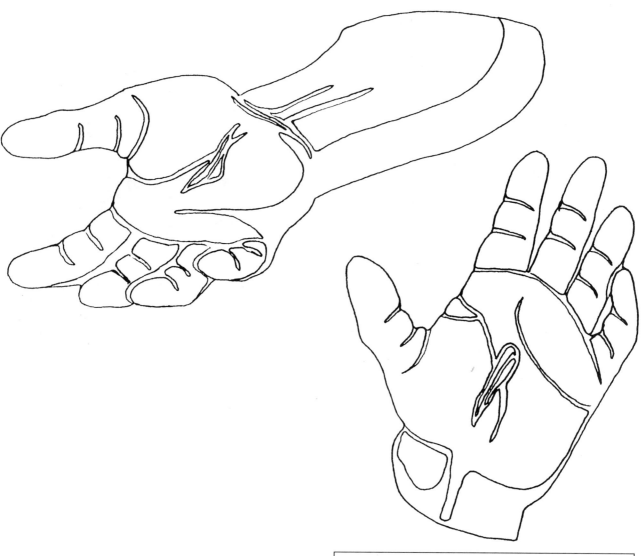

SUGGESTED FABRIC AND COLORS FOR THE HANDS

- Use a medium brown suede-like fabric for the outline fabric.

- Make the hands from a light brown suede-like fabric.

- Make the nail imprints from burgundy and red satin. (The smaller section in each "wound" should be made from the burgundy fabric.) On the left hand, the area between the ring finger and the pinky finger is cut out to reveal the yellow background fabric (see diagram 6).

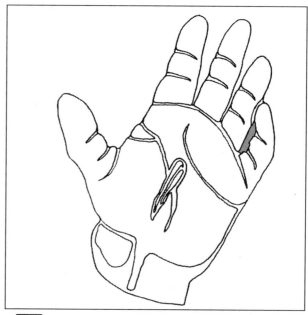

6 *This cutout section reveals the background fabric.*

72

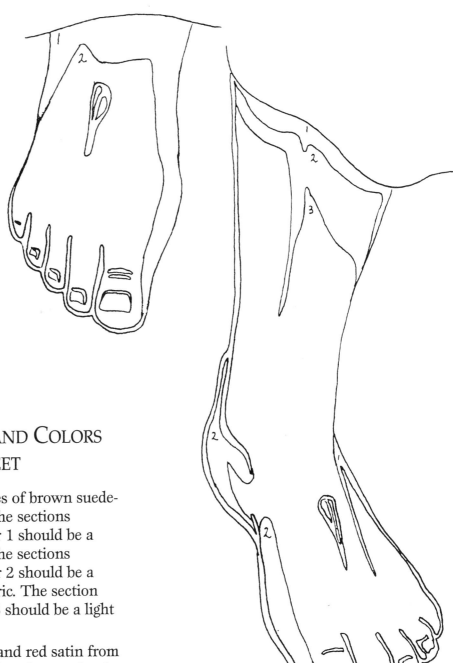

Suggested Fabric and Colors for the Feet

- Use three different shades of brown suede-like fabric for the feet. The sections marked with the number 1 should be a medium brown fabric. The sections marked with the number 2 should be a medium light brown fabric. The section marked with a number 3 should be a light brown fabric.

- Use the same burgundy and red satin from the nail imprints on the hands to make the nail imprints on the feet. The wound shape is a cutout that reveals the brown outline fabric beneath. The satin pieces are placed inside the larger cutout.

- For the toenails on the right foot and the toenail on the big toe of the left foot, use a light brown suede-like fabric. The highlights and creases in the big toe of the right foot are cutouts that reveal the brown outline fabric.

73

ASSEMBLING THE BANNER

Prepare the pattern pieces for the outline fabric of the head; hands; feet; the right sleeve, upper body, and right hip section; the sash; the left sleeve; and the lower garment. (There should be nine outline pieces.) These outline pieces follow the outer edges of the shapes, not all the individual folds and creases. Bond the outline patterns to the appropriate fabrics and iron them in position on the background fabric.

Prepare the pattern for the right sleeve and upper body of the garment (see diagram 7). This piece does not connect to the right hip section or to the belt. As you trace this pattern piece, you will follow each line down the folds and creases. Trace all the cutout sections. Don't forget the triangular piece that is not connected (in the right armpit). Prepare the pattern for the sash (see diagram 8), the lower garment (see diagram 9), the belt (see diagram 10), and the left sleeve (see diagram 11) with the same careful attention to the cutouts.

Bond all the body patterns to the appropriate fabric and lay in position on the outline fabric. Adjust the fit as necessary and tack in position. When you are satisfied with the positioning and the fit of the individual pieces, place a sheet of used HeatnBond paper shiny side down and secure all the design elements.

Next prepare the individual design elements of the face. Once the elements are prepared, tack the hair sections in position. Then place the large oval of the face and the neck section in position. Tack in place. Tack the forehead and nose piece, the eye highlights, the cheekbone sections, the nostrils, and the lower lip highlight in position. Then build the beard and eyebrows and position the inside of the nostrils (Don't forget that the dark brown piece lies under the mustache portion of the beard.) Tack the teeth in place. Finally, build the eyes. The first layer is the off-white eye, then the black outer ring, the brown inner circle, and finally the copper metallic iris highlight. Place

7 *The "shape" of the sleeve and body of the garment. The shaded section is white satin.*

8 *The "shape" of the sash. The black section is light burgundy. The white section is medium burgundy (the outline fabric). The three gray areas are dark burgundy.*

74

a sheet of used HeatnBond paper shiny side down over the face and bond all the design elements securely.

To construct the hands, prepare the pattern pieces and bond them to the appropriate fabric. Be careful as you cut out the creases. There are five separate pieces for each hand (not including the wound pieces). Tack each piece in position (including the fabric pieces that form the nail imprints) and check for fit. Then bond in place.

To construct the feet, prepare the pattern pieces and bond them to the appropriate fabric. Be careful as you cut out the creases. Position them on the background fabric, check for fit, and bond them in place.

Finally, position the outline fabric of the letters. Allow your eye to adjust the spacing between the letters and words. Bond these to the background. Place the decorative fabric on the letter outlines and bond in position.

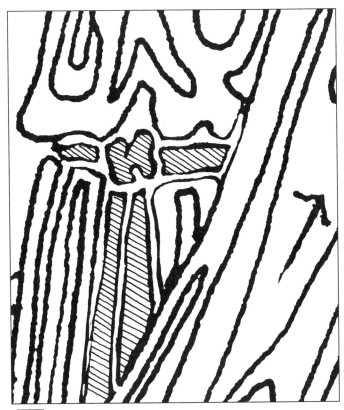

10 *The "shape" of the belt.*

9 *The "shape" of the lower garment. The shaded section is white satin.*

11 *The "shape" of the left sleeve. The shaded section is white satin.*

75

THANKSGIVING BANNER

O give thanks to the Lord for He is good!

SUGGESTED FABRIC AND COLORS

- Use black cotton for the background fabric. If the background fabric is black, there will be no outline fabric. As you adhere the individual design elements, leave a gap between the pieces. If you use a different color for the background, then you will need to cut the outline shape from black cotton.

- Make the pumpkin from dull orange cotton. The center highlight of each section should be a lighter orange cotton. Use light brown cotton for the stem and dark brown cotton for the three highlights. Also use the lighter orange for the portion of the pumpkin that "shows through" the bottle.

- Make the bottle from gray cotton. Use silver lamé for the highlights (the small circle on the body of the bottle, the square on the rim, and the oval on the top).

- Use light pumpkin cotton for the crust of the bread. Use a light chocolate brown suede-like fabric or a chocolate brown leather-like fabric for the highlight sections of the bread crust. The inside of the bread should be an off-white textured cotton with a tone-on-tone print.

- For the flowers, use medium green moiré for the leaves and stem. Use purple or violet satin for the petals and bright yellow satin for the centers of the flowers. (You could use three different shades of violet for the flowers, or you could make one flower violet, one burgundy, and one rust.)

- To construct the Bible, use gold lamé for the page edges. Make the cover from brown cotton. Use red silk for the bookmark. The small triangular sections on either side of the bookmark should be gray cotton. Use bright white satin for the pages (this fabric may need to be lined).

- Use silver lamé for the candlestick holder. Make the candlestick from any color of cotton. The outer flame should be gold lamé and the inner flame silver lamé.

- Use a printed calico cotton in a medium brown shade for the outside of the cornucopia. The interior of the cornucopia should be solid dark brown suede. Make the eggplant from medium purple satin with lavender satin highlights (there are two highlights). The stem and leaf on the eggplant should be green moiré. Make the lemon from a textured yellow silkie (this fabric should be lined) with a light yellow satin highlight. The oranges (between the Bible and the lemon and behind the eggplant) should be made from orange satin (this fabric may need to be lined). Use a lighter shade of orange for the highlight on the orange in the back of the cornucopia. Make the apple from deep red satin with a light red satin highlight. (The half ring around the stem and the section to the left of the stem are cut out from the light red satin to reveal the darker red below.) Make the apple stem from brown cotton. The squash should be a hunter green and yellow calico cotton with a light green cotton highlight.

- Make the bananas from yellow satin. (You can add brown spots with a brown pencil.)

- Use a deep yellow and violet calico cotton for the corn. (Look in the calico section of the fabric store for other printed cottons that might resemble Indian corn.) Make the cornhusks from moiré as follows: sections marked with the number 1 should be a straw-colored fabric; sections marked with the number 2 should be a darker color than the other sections. Use a cotton fabric if moiré in these colors is not available.

- Make the basket from a dark to medium brown suede-like fabric.

- Make the letters from a complementary fabric and color. The letters could be outlined, depending on the color of the background fabric.

Special Notes for Making the Design Elements

As you prepare the pattern pieces, keep in mind that the banner design includes the outline for each design element. You would need to trace this outer line to prepare the outline fabric if you were using a background fabric of any color other than black. If you use a black background fabric, then you will only trace the individual design elements and position them on the black background fabric with an even "outline" between the individual pieces.

It is essential that you number the individual pieces and write the numbers on the corresponding section of an intact photocopy of the design. You may want to place the pieces of each section of the design (for example, the pumpkin, the basket, the cornucopia) in a separate plastic bag.

Pay careful attention to the highlight directions, especially on the basket. The highlight direction for the petals, leaves, and pumpkin sections could follow the directions of the "points" of each element.

If you are using a black outline fabric, note that several cutouts need to be made. There is a small one between the rim of the bottle and the pumpkin, two on either side of the bananas, and two on either side of the stem of the flowers.

If you are outlining the letters, prepare the pattern and bond it to the outline fabric. Then trace the letters again, only ⅛" to ¼" smaller. Bond this pattern to the decorative fabric.

Assembling the Banner

If you are using an outline fabric, position it and adhere it to the background fabric. Then carefully position the individual design elements and check for fit. Tack them in place. Place a sheet of used HeatnBond paper shiny side down over the design and adhere the elements, section by section.

If you are placing the individual elements on a black background fabric, begin by placing the sections of the basket. Try to leave a uniform black "outline" between the pieces. Tack in place. Then position the cornucopia and the fruit. Tack in place. Position the bananas, corn, and Bible. Tack in place. Position the candle, pumpkin, bottle, and bread. Tack in place. Finally, position the stem and leaves and build the flowers.

When the individual pieces are in place, check the whole banner for fit, paying careful attention to the black outline between the elements. Is this outline uniform? If not, make adjustments as necessary. When you're satisfied with the positioning, place a sheet of used HeatnBond paper shiny side down over the design and adhere the elements, section by section.

Finally, position the letters. Allow your eye to adjust the spacing between the letters and words. Adhere in position.

Wedding Banner 1: Chi Rho and Eagle

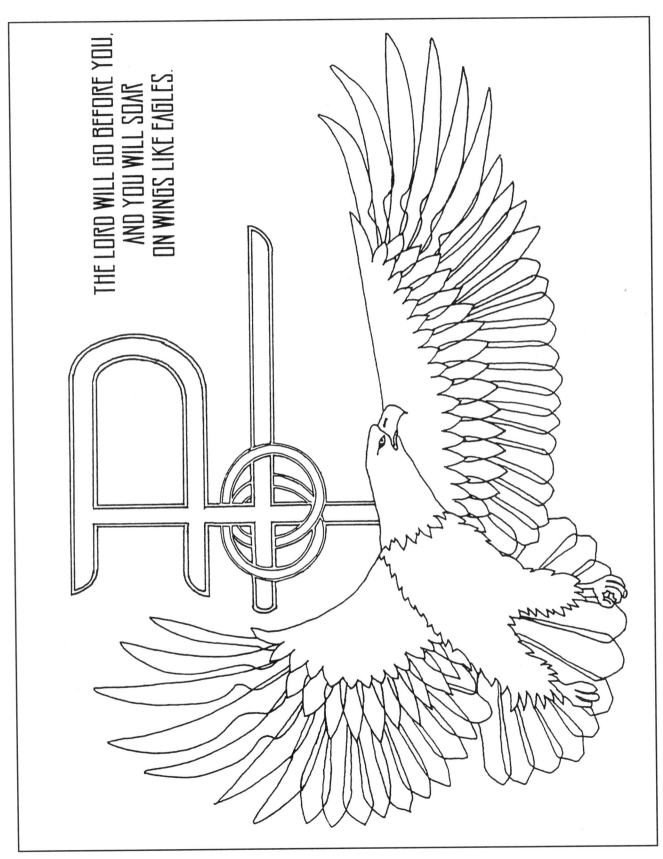

THE LORD WILL GO BEFORE YOU. AND YOU WILL SOAR ON WINGS LIKE EAGLES.

Suggested Fabric and Colors

- For the background fabric, use any color that complements the wedding colors. Do not use white.

- The outline fabric for the Chi Rho and rings, and the eagle's beak, eyes, and feet should be black cotton. There is no outline for the tail feathers or the wings.

- Use a nondirectional gold metallic fabric for the Chi Rho. Make the rings from gold lamé.

- Use a ribbed white satin (with strong directional highlights and shine) for the eagle's head and tail feathers. The feathers on the wings should be brown ribbed satin (with strong directional highlights and shine). Make the feet and beak from mustard yellow satin. The nostril and mouth are made by cutting out the sections from the yellow satin to reveal the black outline fabric. The solid section of the wing and the body should be a damask or upholstery-weight fabric with a feather-like texture. It is best if this fabric is brown to match the satin. However, it can be difficult to match the color so purchase white or off-white fabric and dye it to match the satin (see page 12).

- Use a complementary color for the letters. You can outline the letters with black cotton.

Special Notes for Making the Design Elements

To construct the feet, trace the shape to make the pattern and bond this to the black outline fabric. Then trace the shape again, only ⅛″ to ¼″ smaller. Bond this pattern piece to the mustard yellow fabric. On the right foot, you will need to cut out the section between the talons in both fabrics to reveal the tail feathers below (see diagram 1).

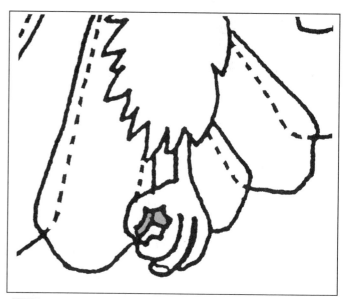

1 *The cutout section in the right foot reveals the tail feathers.*

Make sure you number each design element and the corresponding section on an intact photocopy of the design. This is essential if the wing feathers are to fit together precisely. The highlight of each feather follows the direction of the "point" of the feather.

You may need to line the white fabric used for the head and the tail feathers. Test the white fabric against the outline fabric.

As you prepare the patterns for the individual feathers, you will need to trace the complete feather. This includes the section hidden when the feathers overlap (see diagram 2).

Add ¼″ to the length of each feather at the top edge (where the next layer covers the ends). This will allow you to adjust the layers of the feathers as you build the banner.

If you are outlining the letters, make the patterns for the letters and bond them to the black fabric. Then trace the letters again, only ⅛″ to ¼″ smaller. Bond these patterns to the decorative fabric.

Assembling the Banner

Position the outline fabric for the Chi Rho and rings and the eagle's head on the background fabric. Tack these in position. Then place the solid sections of the wings in place. Check the angles of the wings. Adhere the outline fabric of the Chi Rho and rings and the eagle's head. Tack the wing sections in place, but do not adhere the bottom edges.

Position the white fabric for the head and tack it in place. Do not adhere the bottom edge. Place the body section in position, laying the bottom edge of the head over the top edge of the body. Tack in place. Position the tail feathers under the body section. Make sure the feathers overlap along the edges and create a "fan" shape. The extra length should

help you adjust the shape. As you position each feather, tack it in place at the top. When the tail feathers are in place, gently tack the body over the feathers to help secure them.

Begin positioning the wing feathers of the middle row of feathers from the tip of the wing moving in toward the body. Push the end of each feather under the solid section of the wing. Also overlap the individual feathers. The feathers nearest the body should extend under the body too. Tack each feather in position but do not adhere the bottom edges. Finally, position the longest feathers, again starting at the wing tip and moving in toward the body. Also overlap the individual feathers. The feathers nearest the body overlap the tail feathers and extend under the body. Tack these in place as you position them.

Once the individual feathers are tacked in position, check for placement. Make any corrections, then place a sheet of used HeatnBond paper shiny side down over the design. Adhere the feathers and body parts securely to the background fabric.

Place the eye, beak, and feet design elements in position. Check for fit and adhere the elements. Position the gold fabric for the Chi Rho and rings and iron it in place.

Finally, position the letters. Allow your eye to adjust the spacing between the letters and words. Bond in position. If you are outlining the letters, you could use the black outline to create a shadow effect. Simply bond the black letters in place, then position the decorative letters slightly to the side of the outline letter. Bond in place. You also can add the names of the bride and groom and the wedding date.

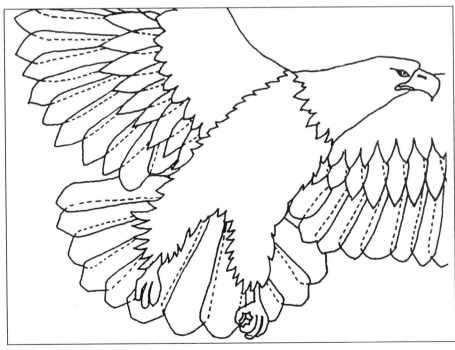

2 *For each feather, trace both the dotted and the dashed lines.*

AND THE TWO SHALL BECOME ONE

SUGGESTED FABRIC AND COLORS

This banner design uses the lacing technique to construct the bunches of grapes on either side of the cross. Review the technique on pages 22–24.

- For the background fabric, use any color that complements the wedding colors. Do not use white.
- Use black cotton for the outline fabric, which includes the tendrils and stems.
- Make the leaves from green moiré.
- Make the grapes from two shades of purple satin—deep purple and medium purple.
- Use medium brown cotton for the vine and light tan cotton for the cross.
- The pages of the Bible should be white satin (this fabric may need to be lined). The page edges should be gold lamé. Make the Bible cover from dark brown suede or from a leather-like fabric. The two small triangular sections on either side of the cross should be medium brown cotton.
- Make the letters from a complementary color.

SPECIAL NOTES FOR MAKING THE DESIGN ELEMENTS

Number each piece and the corresponding section on an intact photocopy of the design. Pay careful attention to the highlight direction.

There are many sections that need to be cut out from the outline fabric to reveal the background fabric. Refer to diagram 1 as you cut out the outline fabric. Cut out the smaller holes with an X-Acto knife before you cut out the larger sections. This will provide extra stability as you work on the smaller holes.

Construct the grape clusters and set them aside.

1 *Pay careful attention to the cutout sections in the outline fabric.*

ASSEMBLING THE BANNER

Position the outline on the background fabric. Don't force the tendrils and stems to curl. Adhere the outline fabric.

Position the design elements for the Bible, the leaves, the grape vine, and the cross. Check for fit, then adhere in position. Do not adhere the grape clusters at this time.

Position the grape clusters and adhere to the banner. Do not iron each separate grape. Instead, let the fabric "poof" through the openings in the outline fabric.

Finally, position the letters. Allow your eye to adjust the spacing between the letters and words. Bond in position. You could add the names of the bride and groom and the wedding date.

Wedding Banner 3: Unity Candle and Flowers

AND THE TWO SHALL BECOME ONE

SUGGESTED FABRIC AND COLORS

- For the background fabric, use any color that complements the wedding colors. Or you can use a blue cotton for the background fabric.

- Use black, navy blue, or hunter green for the outline fabric. (Coordinate this with the colors in the wedding or the church.)

- Make the large background rays from pale shades of blue and white in moirés, smooth and textured satins, silkies, and iridescent lamés.

- Make the leaves shown in diagram 1 from medium dark green cotton. Use emerald green moiré or heavy satin for the rest of the leaves.

- Make the daisy petals from pure white and off-white satin (these fabrics may need to be lined). The petals in the foreground should be made from the pure white fabric (see diagram 2). The centers of the daisies should be a bright yellow textured calico. Use two shades of red silk for the roses. The lighter shade will be used for the five smaller "highlights" on the outermost rose petals (see diagram 3). You also can make the flowers from colors that coordinate with the wedding colors.

- For the ribbon, use an intense color that balances the roses and/or coordinates with the background fabric color. You will need three shades of this color in a satin-like fabric. The lightest shade will be used for the sections marked with an *A*. The medium shade will be used for the sections marked with a *B*. The darkest shade will be used for the sections marked with a *C*. Use the lightest color for the knot.

- Make the candles from white cotton (this fabric may need to be lined). Make the cross from gold lamé (the highlight direction should be vertical). The outer flame

1 *These leaves are made from medium dark green cotton.*

2 *The shaded petals should be made from pure white satin.*

on each candle should be made from gold lamé and the inner flame from silver lamé. Use a gold satin (not a metallic) for the candle stand and a gold lamé for the wedding rings.

- Make the letter outline from a solid cotton that coordinates with the background fabric or with the wedding colors. Use a gold metallic or lamé for the decorative fabric.

SPECIAL NOTES FOR MAKING THE DESIGN ELEMENTS

Make sure you number each design element and the corresponding section on an intact photocopy of the design. Also pay careful attention to highlight direction.

When making the patterns for the background rays, make each ray 1″ longer. This will help you to align the rays when building the banner. Remember the edges will need to butt up against each other but not overlap. The rays are solid pieces of fabric that extend from behind the cross to the banner edge. Other design elements are layered on top of the rays.

The highlight direction for the flowers is difficult to show in such a complex pattern. For the daisies, the highlight on the pure white petals should follow the point of the petal. For the off-white petals, the highlight should run across the width of the petal. See diagram 4 for the highlight directions for the individual sections of the roses.

3 *The highlight scheme for the roses.*

4 *The highlight direction varies for each petal of the roses.*

86

5 *The shaded areas are cutout sections in the outline fabric.*

There are several small cutouts in the outline fabric. There are two cutouts on either side of the base of the center candle immediately above the rings. These cutouts will reveal the background ray behind the center candle. There are also six cutouts in the bouquet (see diagram 5).

When making the letters, first trace the letters and bond the patterns to the outline fabric. Then trace the letters again, only ⅛″ to ¼″ smaller. Bond these patterns to the decorative fabric.

ASSEMBLING THE BANNER

Position the outline fabric and tack it in place on the background fabric. Do not adhere the outline fabric. You will be placing the background rays under this outline fabric.

Lay the flame of the center candle in position. Build the background rays around the flame. As you position the rays, lift the outline fabric to run the ray underneath. Make sure all the rays butt up against each other but do not overlap. Once the rays are correctly positioned, adhere the rays to the background fabric. Move the outline fabric to adhere rays that run beneath it.

Next, position the flames on the two side candles. Place the rays around these candles in the same way you did the background rays. Once you are satisfied with placement, adhere them to the background. Move the outline fabric to adhere the smaller rays that run beneath it. Then adhere the outline fabric.

Build the candles, flames, cross, and candle stand pieces on top of the outline fabric. Adhere these design elements in position.

Next, build the bouquet. Begin by placing the pieces around the edges first. Tack these pieces in position. Then fill in the rest of the bouquet, tacking petals and leaves in place. Once everything is in place, check for fit and make any necessary corrections. Then adhere the design elements to the outline fabric. Adhere the rose highlights last.

Finally, position the outline letters. Allow your eye to adjust the spacing between letters and words. Bond these in position. Then bond the decorative letters on top of the outline fabric. You can bond these decorative letters slightly off center to the outline letters for a shadow effect. You also could add the names of the bride and groom and the wedding date.

PERSONALIZED BANNERS

The following three designs can be personalized and used in combination with the baptism, confirmation, and funeral banners. Use colors that complement the full-size banners when constructing these smaller, personal banners. These smaller banners also provide excellent practice designs.

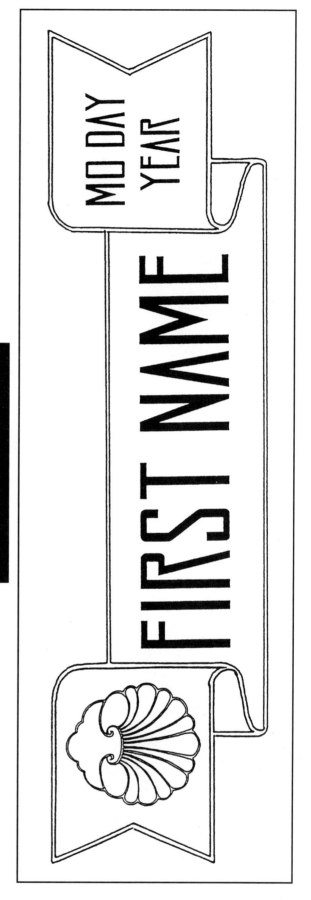

FIRST NAME

MO DAY YEAR

Therefore, if anyone is in Christ, he is a new creation; the old is gone, the new is come!   II Cor. 5:17

ABCDEFGHIJKL
MNOPQRSTUVWX
YZ

abcdefg hij kl m

nopqrstuvwxyz

1234567890

91

ABCDEFGHI
JKLMNOPQ
RSTUVWXY
Z123456 7
890

A B C D E F G H I J K L M N O

P Q R S T U V W X Y Z a b c

d e f g h i j k l m n o p q r s

t u v w x y z 1 2 3 4 5 6 7

8 9 0

ABCDE
FGHIJK
LMNOP
QRSTU
VWXYZ

a b c d e f
g h i j k l m
n o p q r s
t u v w x y
z 1 2 3 4 5
6 7 8 9 0